UNDERSTANDING EU LAW

Karen Davies, LLB, LLM
Lecturer in Law
Swansea Law School

Cavendish
Publishing
Limited

London • Sydney

First published in Great Britain 2001 by Cavendish Publishing Limited, The Glass House, Wharton Street, London WC1X 9PX, United Kingdom

Telephone: +44 (0)20 7278 8000   Facsimile: +44 (0)20 7278 8080

Email: info@cavendishpublishing.com

Website: www.cavendishpublishing.com

British Library Cataloguing in Publication Data

Davies, Karen
Understanding EU law
1 Law – European Union countries
I Title
341.2'422

ISBN 1 85941 611 X

Printed and bound in Great Britain

Contents

Contents

Table of Cases

Table of Legislation

Glossary

Acquis Communautaire	The body of objectives, substantive rules, policies, laws, rights, remedies and case law fundamental to the development of the Community legal order.
Advocates General	Assistants to the European Court of Justice, having the same status as judges.
Assembly	Original name given to the European Parliament.
Assent procedure	The legislative procedure whereby the Council must obtain the Parliament's agreement before certain important decisions may be taken. Introduced by the SEA.
Budget	The Union's revenue and expenditure. The Commission is responsible for submitting a draft budget annually to the Council, which shares budgetary authority with the Parliament.
Charges having equivalent effect	Charges having an equivalent effect to customs duties and, as such, prohibited by Community law.
Citizenship	Citizenship of the Union is dependent on holding nationality of one of the Member States (Art 17 of the EC Treaty).
Co-decision procedure	The legislative procedure whereby the European Parliament is given the power to adopt acts jointly with the Council. Introduced by the TEU (Art 251 of the EC Treaty).
Comitology	The process by which the Commission is assisted by committees in the implementation of legislation.

Committee of the
Regions
The European Union's youngest institution whose birth reflects Member States' strong desire not only to respect regional and local identities and prerogatives, but also to involve them in the development and implementation of EU policies.

Common customs tariff
The common customs duty encircling the Community, charged at the same level no matter where a product is cleared for customs (Arts 23–26 of the EC Treaty).

Common policies
Includes common policies on agriculture, commerce and transport, established to ensure common principles and aims throughout the Community.

Community law
The rules of the Community legal order including primary and secondary legislation, general principles of law and case law of the European Court of Justice. Also known as the *acquis*.

Community competence
The Community is based on the principle of limited powers which are specifically attributed to it by the Treaties. Before the Community may take action, it must ensure that it has been provided with the authority to do so.

Competition rules
Community rules intended to ensure that Competition in the Community is not distorted.

Conciliation Committee
Conciliation Committees may be set up under the co-decision (legislative) procedure with the aim of reaching agreement between the Council and the Parliament in relation to a legislative proposal (Art 251 of the EC Treaty).

Consultation procedure
A legislative procedure under which the Council is bound to consult with the European Parliament and take its views into account.

Consumer protection
Inserted by the TEU, it is intended to promote consumer health, safety, economic and legal interest, and their right to information (Art 153 of the EC Treaty).

Convergence criteria	Criteria that must be attained by those Member States wishing to join the European Single Currency.
Co-operation procedure	A legislative procedure, introduced by the SEA, giving Parliament greater influence in the creation of Community legislation.
COREPER	Name commonly given to the Committee of Permanent Representatives who carry out tasks on behalf of the Council. They also provide a forum in which legislation can be discussed and agreed.
Council of the European Union	More usually known as the Council of Ministers, it has no equivalent anywhere in the world. It is here that the Member States legislate for the Union, set its political objectives, co-ordinate their national policies and resolve differences between themselves and with other institutions.
Court of Auditors	The taxpayers' representative, responsible for checking that the European Union spends its money according to its budgetary rules and regulations and for the purposes for which it is intended.
Court of First Instance	Established by the SEA, the Court has taken over some of the workload of the ECJ, allowing that Court to concentrate on its fundamental task of ensuring the uniform interpretation of Community law.
Court of Justice	Provides the judicial safeguards necessary to ensure that the law is observed in the interpretation and application of the Treaties and, generally, in all of the activities of the Union.
Customs Union	An area where barriers to trade have been eliminated, as exists between the Member States (Arts 23–27 of the EC Treaty).
Decisions	Community legislative acts which are binding upon those to whom they are addressed (Art 249 of the EC Treaty).

Deepening	The process of increased integration between the Member States.
Democratic deficit	Criticism levied at the Community in relation to its perceived remoteness from the ordinary citizen, particularly in relation to the creation of legislation.
Decision making	The processes by which decisions are taking or legislative acts are created within the Community/Union.
Direct applicability	A directly applicable provision of European law is one which takes effect within the Member States without the need for incorporation or implementation by national authorities.
Direct effect	A doctrine established by the European Court of Justice providing that Community law may provide rights and obligations to individuals, enforceable in national courts.
Direct elections	Democratic elections held to elect the Members of the European Parliament (MEPs) (Art 190 of the EC Treaty).
Directives	Legislative acts that oblige Member States to implement the aims contained within the directive by a stipulated date.
Distinctly applicable measure (DAM)	Term used to describe restrictive measures, enacted by Member States, which discriminate between nationally produced goods and those originating in other States.
Dualist State	A State, such as the UK, in which international law and national law are considered distinct and separate from one another.
Economic and Monetary Union	The process whereby the economic and monetary policies of the Member States are harmonised and culminating in the introduction of a single currency.

Economic and Social Committee	In accordance with the Treaties, the Committee advises the Commission, the Council and the European Parliament. The opinions which it delivers (either in response to a referral or on its own initiative) are drawn up by representatives of the various categories of economic and social activity in the European Union.
Effet utile	A principle of law developed by the European Court of Justice to ensure effective enforcement of Community rules within the Member States.
Enlargement	*See* Widening.
Euratom	European Community created in 1957 in order to integrate the nuclear industries of the Member States, promoting safety, research, etc.
European Central Bank	The decision making body in relation to European Monetary Union, responsible for implementing the monetary policy of the Union.
European Coal and Steel Community	European Community created in 1951 in order to integrate the coal and steel industries of the Member States.
European Commission	A Community institutions which has three distinct functions: initiator of proposals for legislation, guardian of the Treaties, and the manager and executor of Union policies and of international trade relations.
European Community (EC)	Community created in 1957 by the Treaty of Rome. Once named the European Economic Community (renamed by the TEU) in order to integrate the economies of the Member States (see Art 2 of the EC Treaty and the Preamble to the EC Treaty).
European Communities	Pillar I of the European Union, comprising the EC, ECSC and Euratom.

European Communities Act	Enacted in the UK in 1972 in order to incorporate the law of the European Community into the law of the UK.
Euro	European unit of currency.
European Convention on Human Rights	Signed under the aegis of the Council of Europe. While the Community/Union has not acceded to the Convention, respect for fundamental human rights has been formalised by the Treaty of Amsterdam.
European Council	The name given to the meetings of the Heads of State of the Member States. Over the last two decades, its summit meetings have played a crucial role in the development of the EU.
European Investment Bank	European Union's financing institution, it provides loans for capital investment, promoting the Union's balanced economic development and integration.
European Parliament	The directly elected democratic expression of the political will of the peoples of the European Union, the largest multinational Parliament in the world.
General principles	A body of unwritten principles supplementing Community legislation and developed by the ECJ from the threads found in the Treaties, the laws of the Member States and international law.
Harmonisation	The process of approximation laws throughout the Member States in order to ensure the establishment and effective functioning of the Internal Market.
High Authority	Original name for what has become the European Commission.
Indirect effect	Doctrine developed by the ECJ requiring national courts to interpret national legislation in the light of European directives.

Indistinctly applicable measure (IDAM)	Restrictive measures enacted by Member States, which apply equally to domestically produced goods and those produced in other states.
Institutions	Five institutions that have been afforded powers by the Treaties in order to ensure aims set out in the EC Treaty are realised (Art 7).
Intergovernmental Conference	Conferences of the Heads of State of the Member States held with the specific purpose of amending the primary legislation of the EC/EU.
Intergovernmentalism	A theory of integration under which the Member States take decisions by co-operation and consensus.
Internal Market	The creation of an internal market is the first of three stages in the creation of an European Union, the others being monetary and political union. It involves uniting the markets of the Member States into a single economic area without internal frontiers.
Judicial Review	Term commonly used to describe the various actions available to the ECJ in order to review the legality of acts of the institutions.
Luxembourg Accords/ Compromise	Agreement reached, in 1966, following the French refusal to accept majority voting in the Council. It allowed Member States to request that decisions be reached by unanimity, rather than majority, when an issue was considered to be of major national interest.
Measures having equivalent effect	Measures having an equivalent effect to quantitative restrictions on trade and held to include state measures which discriminate against imports (DAMs) and those which treat imports and domestic goods alike (IDAMs).
Monist State	A State in which international law is incorporated into the national legal system as soon as it is ratified.

Multi-speed Europe	A term used to describe the system whereby a group of Member States is willing to make an advance in the assumption that other States will follow later. Also known as 'variable geometry'.
Official Journal	A publication of the European Community in which Regulations and Directives must be published, together with other legislative and non-binding acts.
Ombudsman	Every citizen of each Member State is both a national and an European citizen. One of the rights of all European citizens is to apply to the European Ombudsman if they are victims of an act of 'maladministration' by the institutions or bodies.
Pillars of the European Union	The EU is said to be made up of three pillars of which the European Communities comprise the first pillar, common foreign and security policy the second, whilst police and judicial co-operation in criminal matters forms the third.
Preliminary reference	A term describing the procedure by which national courts may request a ruling from the ECJ on the interpretation of primary and secondary Community legislation and on the validity of secondary legislation (Art 234 of the EC Treaty).
Qualified majority voting	A procedure for reaching agreement in Council by which each Member State's votes are weighted to reflect the population of that State (Art 205 of the EC Treaty).
Quantitative restriction	Non-pecuniary restrictions placed on goods by virtue of their crossing a frontier, for example, quotas and total bans.
Regulations	Legislative acts of the institutions of the Community which take effect in all Member States without the need for enacting measures on the part of those States.

Schengen Agreement	An agreement between a number of Member States to abolish checks at common borders in order to achieve free movement of persons.
Soft law	Rules which have no binding force, but which may nevertheless have practical effects.
Single European Act	Amending Treaty signed in 1986 by the Member States. Its main aim was to speed up integration in Community and it also laid down provisions relating to political co-operation.
Supranationalism	A theory of integration involving power moving from the Member States to the Institutions.
Subsidiarity	A principle ensuring that decisions are taken as closely as possible to the citizen in areas which are not in the exclusive competence of the Community/Union.
Supremacy	A doctrine developed by the ECJ, providing that, where Community law and national law conflict, Community law will take precedence.
Transparency	A term used by the institutions to denote openness in their workings. It includes a commitment to access to information (Art 255 of the EC Treaty).
Treaty of Amsterdam	An amending treaty introduced in 1999. Its main aims are to place the interests of workers and citizens at the heart of the Union, to remove existing barriers to free movement while improving security, give the Union a greater voice on the World stage and ensure that the institutions are as effective and efficient as possible in preparation for enlargement.
Treaty on European Union	Signed in 1992, the Treaty not only amended the EC Treaty, but also created the European Union of which the European Communities form a part.

Variable Geometry	*See* Multi-speed Europe.
Widening	A term used to describe the enlargement of the European Community/Union. At present, a number of former Eastern bloc countries are attempting to attain the necessary criteria, together with Malta, Cyprus and Turkey.

Abbreviations

AG	Advocate General
CCT	common customs tariff
CFI	Court of First Instance
CHEE	charge having equivalent effect
CMLR	Common Market Law Review
CoA	Court of Auditors
CoR	Committee of Regions
COREPER	Committee of Permanent Representatives
CU	Customs Union
DAM	distinctly applicable measure
DG	directorate-general
EC	European Community/Treaty Establishing the European Community
ECB	European Central Bank
ECHR	European Convention for the Protection of Human Rights and Fundamental Freedoms/European Court of Human Rights
ECJ	European Court of Justice
ECOSOC	Economic and Social Committee
ECR	European Court Reports
ECSC	European Coal and Steel Community
EEC	European Economic Community
EIB	European Investment Bank
EMU	European Monetary Union
EP	European Parliament

ESCB	European System of Central Banks
ET	employment tribunal
EU	European Union
Euratom	European Atomic Energy Community
IDAM	indistinctly applicable measure
IGC	intergovernmental conference
IPR	intellectual property right
MEP	Member of the European Parliament
MHEE	measure having equivalent effect
NATO	North Atlantic Treaty Organisation
OEEC	Organisation for Economic Co-operation
OJ	Official Journal
QMV	Qualified majority voting
RGM	relevant geographical market
RPM	relevant product market
SEA	Single European Act 1986
TEU	Treaty on European Union 1992
ToA	Treaty of Amsterdam 1997
ToN	Treaty of Nice 2000

1 Introduction

THE SIGNIFICANCE OF EUROPEAN LAW

The UK's membership of the European Community (EC), which itself is now part of a European Union (EU), means that European law has become an integral part of the law of the UK. Knowledge and understanding of the law of the Community is therefore indispensable to all British lawyers.

THE AIMS OF THIS BOOK

In recognition of the importance of European law, it is vital that law students have a solid grounding in its principles. Many students appear, however, to find the study of Community law rather alarming, which is perhaps understandable given the differences of approach and language that exist between the Community's legal system and that of the UK.

Students of European law should, however, take heart. The main body of Community law goes back less than 50 years and has, generally, developed with a set of specific aims in mind, which means that it is possible to approach it in a logical, incremental manner. That is not to say that the scope of EC law is narrow. Indeed, it is not and it would be impossible to cover all that it encompasses, in any degree of depth, in a single volume.

In recognition of the breadth of Community law, the content of most European law courses is necessarily (and thankfully) limited to the principal constitutional and institutional areas of the Community legal order, together with selected areas of substantive law.

Despite this approach, there are still huge areas of law to cover and although there are a number of excellent textbooks providing detailed accounts of the law, such texts can be intimidating or overpowering and, consequently, rather daunting to the new student.

While this book aims to provide an account of the same constitutional and institutional principles, together with important areas of substantive law, albeit in a less circuitous manner than many texts, a different approach has been taken. At the beginning of each topic, before the legal principles are examined, each area of law is put into context, thus allowing an *understanding* of relevant issues to be developed.

In addition, at the end of most sections, knowledge and understanding are consolidated by the provision of diagrams and/or flowcharts that clearly highlight the *main* points at issue.

This approach is intended to encourage an understanding of European law as a whole, allowing students to develop a 'feel' for the subject and, ultimately, resulting in far less rote learning being necessary just before examinations!

HOW TO STUDY EU LAW

One's approach to studying European law can undoubtedly make all the difference to one's enjoyment of the course and, also, to the end result. The subject of the UK's membership of the European Union is one of keen debate in the media and it is almost impossible not to have formed some sort of opinion as to whether Britain should be 'in' or 'out'! Certain UK newspapers appear to thrive on discussion as to whether Europe should dictate the shape of the bananas we eat and whether hedgehog flavoured crisps should be banned, and it is often difficult to arrive at the study of European law with an open mind. But this is an essential pre-requisite to successful study!

During your course you will be expected to attend lectures and tutorials. Do not underestimate the importance of these. We all learn in various ways, not only through what we read, but also by listening, seeing and doing. Reading various texts, periodicals etc is essential, but attending lectures can focus the mind, provide an introduction to a topic, shed light on areas of confusion and afford an alternative point of view!

Similarly, tutorial attendance has numerous advantages (and attendance is often mandatory if you wish to stay on the course!). It allows various topics or points to be focused upon, it provides opportunity for discussion, it allows for clarification and may also provide practice in answering essays, exam-type questions and providing legal advice. Be sure not to miss out on these opportunities.

FINDING OUT ABOUT EUROPEAN LAW

Resources

There is a wealth of sources of information on the European Union and Community law. Those enrolled on a structured course will normally be provided with at least an outline reading list of appropriate textbooks and useful legal journals.

Make sure you have an up to date copy of EC legislation at the start of your course. If used regularly, you will find such a text invaluable. The EC Treaty and secondary legislation are, by and large, very readable and you should always read the various Treaty Articles as you study them.

In addition to these traditional sources of legal information, Internet access has opened up a huge source of materials. The number of web sites containing information on Community law appears to grow daily and it is a virtually impossible task to provide a comprehensive list. The European Union does however have its own site, which is a good place to begin as it also provides a number of links to other relevant sites. The address of this site is **http://europa.eu.int/abc/obj/amst/en/index.htm**

In addition, the Community institutions produce a wealth of literature, and even CD-ROMs, on various aspects of the European Community and European Union, much of which is *free*. A list of such publications, together with details of how to order can be found on the above website.

BEGINNING YOUR STUDIES

Coping with jargon

Law students often remark that, when they embark on a course of study of a particular branch of law, not only do they have to take on board new legal principles, statutes, case law, etc, but that they also have to cope with legal jargon that is particular to that area of law. This is certainly true of European law and students new to the subject may find themselves confused by terminology.

In order to overcome this problem, which can have serious consequences, as students who fail to break through the jargon may never fully understand the law beyond, this book provides a glossary of commonly used terms. It is advisable to glance through this glossary at the *beginning* of any course of study and it should be regularly referred to throughout.

One important piece of terminology that needs to be understood from the outset is the difference between the *European Community* and the *European Union*. The terms are often used interchangeably, yet they are very different. As you will soon discover, the European Community, once known as the European Economic Community, was created under the Treaty of Rome by its six original members in 1957. The European Union was, on the other hand, created by the Treaty on European Union, in 1992. The confusion arises because the EU is a complex structure made up of a number of parts, one of which is the EC. The EC is therefore part of the EU, but not the same as it! This should become clearer once Chapter 2, entitled 'The Creation of a European Union', has been read and digested.

Dealing with case names

In addition to the often oblique terminology which has been adopted by European lawyers, students of EC law often find the names of the decisions of the European Court of Justice to be a nightmare!

When it is considered that the EU is comprised of 15 states and has 11 official languages, it is understandable that case names should occasionally prove difficult to pronounce and spell. Few lawyers would pretend that Case 109/88, *Handels-OG Kontorfunktionaernesforbund v Dansk Arbeejdsgiverforening,* flows easily off either the tongue or the pen. Despair may be avoided, however, once one understands that many EC law cases have nicknames that are often acceptable for use in examinations (but do check with your tutor). For example, the commonly used and accepted nickname for the above case is *Danfloss* which, I am sure you will agree, is quite manageable!

In the table of cases at the beginning of this book, you will find that the common nicknames of most cases have been included.

Making sure you know 'which way you are going'

Life can be made far easier if we know which direction we are going in. If we are unsure, then life can be very confusing. The same can be said of studying European law. It is not sufficient to know that you are going to

4

study EC law. In order to make studying as painless as possible, and even enjoyable, you need to have some knowledge of precisely what areas of law you are going to study *and why* and, also, in what order various topics are going to be considered.

If you are provided with a course guide or timetable, such information is often contained within it. Generally, undergraduate EC law courses follow the following scheme.

CONCLUSIONS

Hopefully, this book will not be seen as just another simplified or insubstantial text, but rather as an introduction to European law that

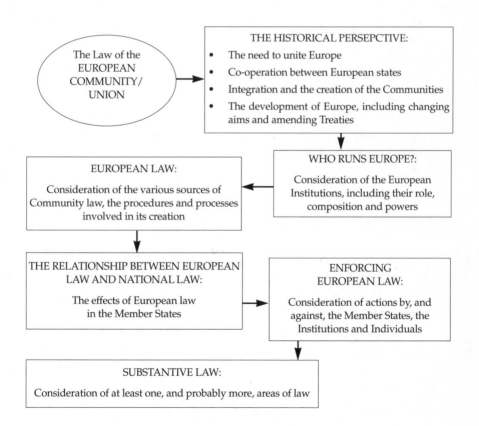

ensures that all who access it provide themselves with firm foundations on which to build greater and deeper knowledge. No strong, high or long lasting wall was ever built without a sound foundation being put in place first!

Remember that this book does not profess to contain all you will need to know about Europe but, hopefully, it will provide the desire and the tools to study further. Finally, if there is something you don't understand, please don't let it blight your studies – if you don't know, find a man (or woman) who does, and ASK! Most tutors worth their salt will be only too pleased to help.

2 The Creation of a European Union

(1) WHY WAS THE EUROPEAN COMMUNITY CREATED?

The best way to understand European law is to start at the beginning, which inevitably involves some consideration of why the Community exists at all. The idea of an united Europe is certainly not a new one and a variety of leaders have, across the centuries, attempted to achieve European integration. With regard to more modern times, it is possible to highlight the end of the Second World War in 1945 as the catalyst which set in motion events that have led to the creation of a European Union.

The economies of the European States had been devastated by war and the peoples of Europe were anxious to build a better and peaceful future for themselves. The United States of America saw a union between the European States as a means of countering a perceived communist threat from the eastern bloc countries and, consequently, provided financial aid, under what became known as the Marshall Plan. In order to administer this programme of aid, the Organisation for Economic Co-operation was set up in 1948, inevitably involving co-operation between recipient States. Other organisations such as the North Atlantic Treaty Organisation (NATO), whose aims primarily related to defence, were also created and can be seen as early forms of modern co-operation in Europe.

The Council of Europe

Further co-operation between European governments led, in 1947, to the creation of the Council of Europe, an intergovernmental organisation which adopted the European Convention on Human Rights and established the European Court of Human Rights. It needs to be emphasised from the outset, however, *that this organisation is totally separate from that which has become known as the European Community/Union.* While undoubtedly performing valuable tasks, particularly in the area of human rights, the

Council of Europe fell short of what many felt was needed in order to stabilise inter-State relationships *and* ensure economic regeneration.

THE FIRST EUROPEAN COMMUNITY – THE EUROPEAN COAL AND STEEL COMMUNITY

A plan based on economic co-operation in Europe was proposed by Jean Monnet and taken up by Robert Schuman, the then French Foreign Minister. This embryonic scheme involved the integration of the French and German coal and steel industries as a means of stabilising the relationship between the two countries. The plan allowed two 'war-making' industries to be monitored, ensuring that the capacity of the parties to secretly re-arm was reduced. However, as the idea also included ensuring security on a wider European scale, an invitation to participate was proffered to other countries and the European Coal and Steel Community (ECSC) was finally created by the signing of the Treaty of Paris in 1951. This new Community had an initial membership of six, namely France, Germany, Italy, Belgium, Luxembourg and the Netherlands (the then British Prime Minister, Sir Anthony Eden, had declared that the UK had no need to join, as it was well able to 'stand on its own two feet' – a reference to the UK's links with both the Commonwealth and the USA).

The creation of the ECSC was particularly significant, as it moved away from the more traditional intergovernmental system of co-operation between participating States. Four independent institutions were created to run the Community and the power to control the coal and steel industries was moved from the participating States to these institutions, which comprised a High Authority, an Assembly, a Council and a Court of Justice. The new Community consequently had a decidedly supranational, rather than intergovernmental, flavour. It is interesting to note that, although 50 years have gone by since this transfer of 'sovereign powers' first took place, as we shall see later, the extent of this transfer of authority still remains a matter of debate and contention within the European Union.

While the immediate focus of the ECSC was undoubtedly economic, that is, the creation of a common market in coal and steel, with common policies and the removal of all barriers to trade in those commodities, it should not be forgotten that the contracting States saw economic co-operation as a *means to an end*; that is, ensuring that the longer term aims of peace and European unity were achieved. This can be evidenced by reference to the Preamble to the Treaty of Paris which provides that the establishment of an economic community is a *'basis for a broader and deeper community among peoples long divided by bloody conflicts; and to lay the foundations for institutions which will give direction to a destiny henceforward shared'*.

THE EUROPEAN ATOMIC ENERGY COMMUNITY

Following the creation of the ECSC, further attempts at integration between the contracting States were made, with plans being drawn up for a European Defence Community and European Political Community, involving the creation of a European army and a common European foreign policy. Agreement could not, however, be reached on these matters and it was not until 1956 that a way forward towards further integration was found. A report was published by an intergovernmental committee chaired by Paul-Henri Spaak, the then Belgian Foreign Minister, detailing plans for a further two communities, the European Atomic Energy Community (Euratom) and the European Economic Community (EEC).

The Euratom Treaty was signed in Rome in 1957 by the same six countries that had previously joined together to form the ECSC. The object of this new Community can be summarised as the furtherance of atomic energy for peaceful purposes, together with a commitment to uniform safety standards. Once more, as for the ECSC, the control of each Member State's atomic industries was passed to four autonomous institutions, with the Assembly and Court of Justice being common to both Communities.

THE EUROPEAN ECONOMIC COMMUNITY

Like Euratom, the EEC was born as a result of the Spaak Report and the Treaty establishing the EEC was signed in Rome by the same six Member States on the same day as the Euratom Treaty. A further similarity lies in the fact that the new Community was to be administered by four independent institutions upon whom the Member States had delegated the right of independent action in certain, specified areas. (Once more, the Court of Justice and the Assembly were shared between the Communities.)

Both the ECSC Treaty and the Euratom Treaty were, however, limited in their scope, in that they had as their aims the creation of a common market in coal and steel and in atomic energy, respectively. The EEC Treaty was significantly *broader* in its approach, in that it was created with the task of working towards integration of *all* aspects of the economies of its Member States, rather than integration of specific industries.

While the vehicle for integration was once more economic, the Preamble to the EEC Treaty of 1957 again suggested that longer term goals were wider, including a determination to '*lay the foundations of an ever closer union among the peoples of Europe*'. This was very much in line with Monnet and Schuman's view that integration of the Member States' economies would spill over into other areas, namely political and social.

(2) THE DEVELOPMENT OF THE EUROPEAN COMMUNITIES

The term 'European Communities' is used to denote all three Communities, that is the ECSC, Euratom and the EEC. This should not be confused with the European Community (EC), which is the *new* name for the EEC as introduced by the Treaty on European Union (discussed below). The Communities have not stood still since their inception and, in order to fully understand their present position, the major milestones in their development need be to be considered.

The Merger Treaty 1965

The Merger Treaty, which came into effect in 1967, was the first amendment to the Treaties of Paris and Rome. Its main purpose was to merge the institutions of all three Communities, creating a common Council of Ministers and a common Commission (formerly known as the High Authority). The remaining two institutions, the European Parliament (EP) (formerly the Assembly) and the Court of Justice already served all three Communities.

Enlargement of the EEC

(a) Britain's membership of the Communities

By the early 1960s, the Member States of the Community were beginning to enjoy the benefits of membership. A number of non-member European States, in particular the UK, were becoming aware of the apparent benefits of membership and, in 1961, Britain made its first application to join. General De Gaulle, the then President of France, made no secret of his hostility towards British membership, feeling instead that the UK should continue its association with the Commonwealth and the USA. Britain's application was consequently rejected. A second UK bid to join, in 1967, also failed. It was not until January 1973, following De Gaulle's resignation, that the UK, together with Ireland and Denmark, was finally admitted.

(b) Further broadening of the Communities

In 1981, Greece joined the Communities, with Portugal and Spain raising the number of Member States to 12 by 1986. Austria, Sweden and Finland joined in January 1995, bringing the total to the present 15 Member States. Norway, Turkey, Morocco, Cyprus and Malta have also applied for membership, but as yet remain outside the Communities. Since 1993, it has been recognised that membership is a goal for a number of former eastern bloc countries, including Hungary, Poland, Romania, the Czech Republic and Bulgaria. Preparation for such enlargement is now underway, although no firm dates have been set as yet.

The Single European Act 1986

The Single European Act (SEA) 1986, which came into effect in 1987, is considered to be the first *substantial* revision of the Treaties. While considerable early success had been enjoyed, with a customs union, for example, being completed ahead of schedule in 1968, progress with regards to further integration had slowed to near stagnation. This near standstill was blamed on a number of factors, both external and internal, including world recession and difficulties relating to decision making within the Community, and the SEA can be viewed as a response to such problems.

The SEA, which is divided into sections known as 'Titles', contains a number of important provisions, both amending the original ECSC,

Euratom and EEC Treaties and also laying down provisions for *political co-operation* between the Member States.

First, under Title I, the new Treaty formalised European political co-operation by recognising the European Council and providing for twice-yearly meetings. (Take care not to confused the European Council with the Council of Ministers, or Council of the European Union as it is now known. The European Council is a separate organisation created in 1974, with a membership composed of the Heads of State or Government of the Member States, foreign ministers and the Commission President.)

Title II amended the existing Treaties and, in an attempt to ensure *increased efficiency and democracy* within the institutional framework, the SEA effected a number of changes. First, a Court of First Instance was created to assist the overworked European Court of Justice (ECJ). In addition, a new legislative procedure, known as 'co-operation', was introduced which provided the Assembly, *renamed the European Parliament*, with increased influence in the legislative process. The Parliament was also given the right of veto over the accession of new Member States.

Changes to the Parliament's functions were a response to calls for an enhanced role following the introduction of *direct elections* for Members of the European Parliament (MEPs), by citizens of the Member States, which had been agreed in 1976. The first elections took place in 1979 and were significant, in that the Parliament became the first Community institution to receive a direct, democratic mandate.

In an attempt to revitalise progress towards economic integration, Title II also introduced the idea of an *'internal market'* to be attained by a set date: 31 December 1992. Also known as the *'single market'*, the internal market was intended to take the Community beyond being merely a customs union (that is, an area without internal barriers to trade) to a Community with complete totality of economic activity.

It was realised that the creation of a single market would require substantial legislative activity by the institutions and, with this in mind, the SEA introduced a change to voting procedures in the Council. The use of *qualified majority voting* (whereby each Council Minister's vote is 'weighted', reflecting the population of the Member State) was significantly increased and, with the corresponding move away from the need for unanimity, the legislative process was effectively speeded up. (It is far easier, and quicker, to ensure majority agreement to a legislative proposal than to achieve unanimity.)

Title II further *extended the existing substantive areas of Community competence*, formally recognising co-operation in economic and monetary union, social policy, economic and social cohesion (that is, reducing disparity between the various regions within the Community), research and technological development and action on protection of the environment.

Finally, Title III referred to *political co-operation*, albeit outside formal Community structures. It provided for the inclusion of the Commission and EP within the process and also for the development of co-operation in foreign policy and security fields. This Title has since been repealed and replaced by more detailed provisions.

While the SEA has not been without its critics, who decried it as vague and ambiguous, it undoubtedly gave renewed momentum to plans for the economic integration of Europe and also laid important foundations for social and political integration. Institutional changes introduced by the Act supported the supranational nature of the Communities by increasing the influence of both the Parliament and the Commission, while, at the same time, qualified majority voting (QMV) was recognised as the norm in Council, decreasing the influence of individual Member States.

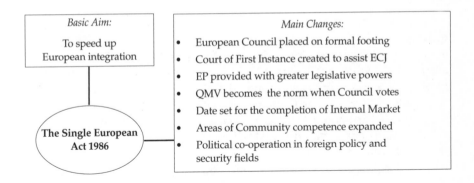

The Treaty on European Union 1992

The Treaty on European Union (TEU), also commonly known as the Maastricht Treaty after the Netherlands town where it was signed, was created with two broad aims in mind. First, to sustain the momentum created by the SEA and, secondly, the creation of a new organisation, albeit founded on the original Communities, to be known as the European Union (EU). The Treaty itself can be divided into two distinct parts, that which *amends* the original Treaties (and in that way it is similar to the SEA) and that which created the EU (in a similar manner to the way in which the Treaty of Paris created the ECSC).

(a) Changes to the original Treaties

The TEU is once more divided into sections or 'Titles', with changes made to the original ECSC, Euratom and, particularly, EEC Treaties contained in Titles II to IV. First, the Treaty *renamed* the European Economic Community the European Community (EC), with the Treaty creating the EEC also being renamed the EC Treaty. It can be argued that the removal of the term 'economic' from the Community's title was intended to indicate that, with the process of economic integration nearing completion, the EC could now begin to concentrate on moving towards further integration in social and political areas.

The TEU also broadened the *aims* of the Community to include such objectives as monetary union and social and environmental protection. In addition, the new Treaty provided for institutional and legislative changes, together with a timetable for the introduction of *European Monetary Union* (EMU). New areas of Community competence were introduced, while others were expanded. While the main changes are highlighted immediately below, they will be further discussed, as appropriate, in later chapters.

The EP's involvement in the *legislative process* was once more increased by extended use of the co-operation procedure (introduced by the SEA) and the introduction of a new procedure known as *co-decision*, which effectively allows the Parliament to 'veto' legislative proposals. In addition, the Parliament was given a right of initiative with regard to legislation, once a monopoly enjoyed by the Commission. The Parliament was also afforded the power to appoint a European *Ombudsman* to investigate complaints relating to alleged maladministration on the part of the Community institutions and their staff.

Other changes involving the institutions included formally recognising the Court of Auditors (CoA) as a Community institution and the creation of a European Central Bank (ECB).

The TEU introduced the concept of European citizenship, which is provided to nationals of the Member States, although such status does not appear to extend their rights or obligations. With regard to issues relating to economic and monetary policy, the path towards EMU, first introduced by the SEA, was further elaborated upon and a timetable set for its various stages, climaxing with the adoption of a single currency. A new timetable for the free movement of capital was also introduced.

With regard to the creation of the European Union, the TEU created a 'three pillared' structure, comprising of:

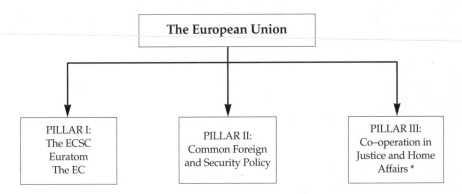

(*Since amended by the Treaty of Amsterdam)

Pillar II, created under Title V of the TEU, provides for the development of policies that relate largely to the Member States and their relationship with the rest of the world. Pillar III, created under Title VI of the TEU, provided for *inter-State co-operation* on policies including asylum, external border controls, immigration and international fraud together with judicial co-operation on civil and criminal matters, and police co-operation relating to terrorism and drugs.

In contrast with the EC, the EU does not have separate legal personality and, with regard to Pillars II and III, *there has been no transfer of sovereign powers from the Member States*. Instead, progress under Pillars II and III can only be achieved through intergovernmental co-operation and consensus amongst all Member States. This does not mean that there is no institutional involvement. While the European Council takes the major political decisions of the EU, the Council of Ministers, which represents the Member States, was provided with a central decision making role. The Parliament was limited to a consultative role (reminiscent of its original role as the Assembly), while the Commission's role was limited to the non-executive right of initiative. As Pillars II and III do not produce legally binding acts (that is, the law of the EU is contained within the 'EC pillar'), the ECJ was left with virtually no role to play under those pillars.

As with the SEA before it, the TEU has been the subject of considerable academic analysis and criticism, not all complimentary. Commentators provide, for example, that the structure of the Union is too complex and fragmented and that the 'opt-outs' available provide for loss of unity (for example, the UK's reluctance to join the single currency). On the other hand, the Treaty has also been praised for measures such as increasing the role of the Parliament, widening the areas of European competence and increased flexibility.

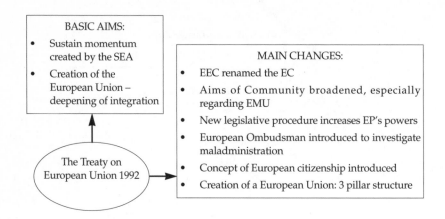

BASIC AIMS:
- Sustain momentum created by the SEA
- Creation of the European Union – deepening of integration

The Treaty on European Union 1992

MAIN CHANGES:
- EEC renamed the EC
- Aims of Community broadened, especially regarding EMU
- New legislative procedure increases EP's powers
- European Ombudsman introduced to investigate maladministration
- Concept of European citizenship introduced
- Creation of a European Union: 3 pillar structure

The Treaty of Amsterdam 1997

The Treaty of Amsterdam (ToA), which came into effect in May 1999, has been described as a consolidating Treaty, its main purposes being to improve processes, increase effectiveness and to bring the EU closer to the ordinary person by making it more comprehensible.

Its general provisions, that is those that effect all three Pillars, include a commitment to greater openness in the decision making processes of the EU and the recognition that the Union is based on respect for human rights, democracy and the rule of law. Indeed, membership of the Union is now contingent upon respect for such principles and the Treaty goes as far as to declare that the Union must respect the fundamental human rights protected under the European Convention on Human Rights. Any Member State found to be in 'serious and persistent' breach of such rights may find its own rights, particularly those in regard to voting, suspended.

The ToA transfers a number of areas previously contained in Pillar III to Pillar I. These areas include issues relating to free movement of persons such as visas, asylum and immigration and also customs co-operation. (It is important to note that the UK and Ireland have negotiated an 'opt-out' and that they, and Denmark, have failed to sign the 1985 Schengen Treaty on the abolition of border checks.) This has resulted in issues relating to the establishment of 'an area of freedom, justice and security' being contained within both Pillars I and III, which has, in turn, led to a blurring of the pillars and also of the role of institutions, particularly the EP and the ECJ.

With regard to Pillar I (the Communities), under the ToA, the EC Treaty was 'tidied up', with all obsolete provisions being removed. This resulted in an almost complete *re-numbering* of the Treaty and *students need to ensure that they know whether Treaty Articles referred to in journals and books relate to the old or new system of numbering.*

Specific changes to the EC Treaty include a new non-discrimination provision that provides the EC with the authority to create legislation aimed at combating discrimination based on sex, racial or ethnic origin, religion or belief, disability, age and/or sexual orientation. Member States are also encouraged to work together to combat unemployment, while issues such as public health and consumer protection have also been amended.

With regard to the institutions, the EP has been allowed yet further involvement in the legislative process as the use of the co-decision procedure, included by virtue of the TEU, has been expanded and streamlined. In *preparation for enlargement* of the Union, membership of the EP has been capped at 700 MEPs, while composition of the Commission is to remain at 20 Commissioners.

In an attempt to stem some of the criticisms levied at the original Pillar II, a number of changes where made to its structure by Title V of the ToA. These largely related to procedures, financing, institutional involvement and international identity, together with a revision of the defence provisions. With regard to Pillar III, amended by Title VI of the ToA, as has already been discussed above, a substantial part of the subject matter of the Pillar has been moved to Pillar I, where it has been included into the EC Treaty. The Pillar has been renamed *Police and Judicial Co-operation in Criminal Matters* with areas targeted for 'common action' including terrorism, drugs and arms trafficking, trafficking in persons, offences

MAIN CHANGES:

- new numbering of EC Treaty
- authority to create legislation aimed at prohibiting discrimination
- greater use of the 'co-decision' legislative procedure
- Pillar III to be renamed 'Police and Judicial Co-operation in Criminal Matters' with consequential changes to pillar content
- EP capped at 700 MEPs and Commission at 20, in preparation for enlargement

BASIC AIMS:

To improve processes, increase effectiveness and bring EU closer to the ordinary citizen, by:

- placing workers and citizens rights at the heart of the Union
- removing remaining barriers to free movement
- preparing for enlargement

The Treaty of Amsterdam 1997

against children, corruption, fraud and the prevention and combating of racism and xenophobia.

The Treaty of Nice 2000

At the time of writing, the Treaty of Nice (ToN) has yet to be ratified and it should consequently be noted that the commentary provided below is based on what was agreed at the Intergovernmental Conference held in Nice in December 2000, rather than on an implemented treaty.

The ToN is intended to *facilitate the enlargement of the European Union* and it is worth spending a moment to consider that the aims of creating and maintaining a stable and prosperous Europe are now about to be embraced by the once isolated countries of eastern Europe. While much has been made of the difficulties experienced by the Member States in reaching agreement as to the content of the new Treaty, all are firmly committed to widening EU membership.

The changes likely to be introduced by Nice have been described at best as modest and even as disappointing, with decision making likely to become less, rather than more, efficient and transparent. It has been argued that important issues such as the future of the Common Agricultural Policy and how power will, in future, be divided by the Member States and Europe have been ignored and it would appear that many significant decisions have been put off until 2004 *when the next IGC will be held.*

The *key points* agreed at Nice can however be summarised as follows:

- extension of *qualified majority voting* within the Council with a consequent decline in the need for unanimity in limited areas;
- *reweighting* of votes in the Council in favour of the larger EU countries;
- *institutional changes*, particularly with regard to the Commission, who will be allowed to increase in size to 26 members, although larger states are set to lose their second Commissioner by 2005. Plans also include major reforms to the organisation of the Commission.

In addition to the above changes, the European Council agreed on a number of other issues including the future status of the EU's Charter of Fundamental Rights as a political document, the adoption of a social agenda and the establishment of a European Food Authority. In was also agreed that the manner in which future summits are organised should be reviewed.

As Romaino Prodi, President of the European Commission, noted in a speech to the European Parliament on 12 December, 2000: '... *the final aim of the Nice Summit was and remains the reunification of Europe. The new Millennium has given us an unprecedented opportunity to bind together the countries of our continent into a wide area of peace, stability and greater economic potential. Nice is a step in this direction.*'

(3) THE EUROPEAN UNION TODAY

It should be evident by this stage that the present European Union is a complex structure. The Member States, while all subscribing to the idea of an integrated Europe, do not always agree on the extent of such integration or on the means by which it may be achieved. The original European Community, the ECSC created in 1952, was designed as a first step in achieving lasting peace and increasing prosperity in a continent scarred by war which, by and large, has been achieved. However, the aims and objectives of the Union are constantly developing in response to both internal and external stimuli and the integration of Europe is far from complete.

Enlargement of the Union is on the horizon and that in itself presents tremendous challenges. The ambitious target of introducing a single currency throughout the Union is still near the top of any European agenda as is the deepening of European integration to include both wider political and social issues. The Union is also striving to establish its own global identity. The only thing that can be asserted with complete authority is that it is impossible to predict with any certainty what the future shape of Europe will be.

Important dates and events in the creation of a European Union

Apr 1951	Six European States sign the Treaty of Paris establishing the ECSC
Mar 1957	The six sign the two Treaties of Rome establishing Euratom and the EEC
Jan 1958	Treaties of Rome come into force
Apr 1965	Merger Treaty is signed providing all three Communities with the same institutional structure
Jul 1967	Merger Treaty enters into force
Apr 1970	First Budgetary Treaty signed, making major changes to the funding of the Communities
Jan 1973	Denmark, Ireland and the UK join the Community
Dec 1974	European Council agrees on direct elections for the EP – a major step in ensuring democratic governance of Europe
Jul 1975	Second Budgetary Treaty signed
Jul 1978	European Council agrees on closer monetary co-operation
Jun 1979	First direct elections of the EP
Jan 1981	Greece joins the Community
Jan 1986	Spain joins the Community
Feb 1986	SEA signed with the aim of speeding up European integration
Jul 1987	SEA enters into force
Jul 1989	Austria joins Community
Feb 1992	TEU signed in Maastricht – creates a European Union
Nov 1993	TEU enters into force
Jan 1995	Austria, Finland and Sweden join the Union
Oct 1997	ToA signed – consolidating Treaty aimed at improving processes and efficiency and also bringing EU closer to its citizens
May 1999	ToA enters into force
Dec 2000	ToN signed

3 Who Runs Europe?

(1) POWER SHARING

Since the first European Coal and Steel Community (ECSC), was created, the Member States have delegated powers to a number of institutions who 'run' the Communities on their behalf. Together, these institutions form the Government of the European Union (EU), taking decisions, creating laws and spending money on a joint (Community), rather than individual (State) basis, *but only in areas in which they have been provided with the authority so to do.* The Member States still retain the power to create and amend the constitutional rules of the EU, as has been done through a variety of Treaties, such as the Single European Act (SEA), Treaty of European Union (TEU) and Treaty of Amsterdam (ToA), and they continue to be solely responsible in areas that lie outside the competence of the EC.

Over the past 50 years, numerous theories of integration have been put forward in an attempt to explain *how* power is, or should be, shared between the Member States and the institutions. *Federalism* has proved a tremendous influence on the governance of the EC. Although there is no precise agreed definition of federalism, and a cursory examination of various federal systems throughout the world reveals that there are many different models, it basically means that there is a dispersal of power between different levels of government.

Federalist ideas are evident throughout the Treaties, with great emphasis begin placed on the EC institutions which enjoy a large degree of autonomy in specific fields. A federalist principle that has proved important to the EC is that of *subsidiarity*. The principle, which was given formal recognition by the TEU, can now be found in Art 5 of the EC Treaty. It provides that decisions should be taken at the *most appropriate level*, as close to the citizen as possible, demonstrating that power is intended to be shared between the supranational institutions, national (Member State) and sub-national (regional) levels.

The idea of a federal Europe has, however, not proved popular with all Member States, the UK included, due to the necessity of surrendering sovereignty, albeit in limited fields. An alternative theory of integration is that of *intergovernmentalism*. This term describes a power sharing arrangement that allows Member States to collaborate whilst still retaining sovereignty. Intergovernmentalism has been criticised, due to its tendency to promote the interests of individual States, rather than Europe as a whole and, also, due to the difficulties often encountered in reaching agreement between the Member States. The EU can be seen as embracing both theories of integration. While Pillar I (EC) relies largely on its supranational institutions to take decisions that bind the Member States, decisions relating to Pillars II and III are reached by the Member States acting together on an intergovernmental basis, with limited involvement from the institutions other than the Council.

(2)   THE INSTITUTIONAL STRUCTURE

The Institutions and other Community bodies

Article 7 of the EC Treaty provides that the tasks entrusted to the Community shall be carried out by *five* institutions, namely the European Parliament (EP), the Council, the Commission, the European Court of Justice (ECJ) and the Court of Auditors (CoA). The Treaties have also provided for the establishment of several additional bodies such as the European Council, the Economic and Social Committee (ECOSOC) and the Committee of the Regions. As the Communities have grown and developed into the EU, so, too, have the institutions grown and developed. In order to ensure that no one body becomes too powerful, thereby disturbing the delicate balance that exists between the various interests within the Union, a number of checks and balances are inbuilt into the European Union's system of governance.

In order to understand the workings of the institutions, each will be considered separately in terms of the role that it plays and also with regard to its relationship with the other institutions.

The functions of government

Before embarking on such considerations, it is worth taking a moment to remind ourselves of the traditional division of government functions, that is, legislative, executive and judicial. In the UK, an attempt is made at keeping each area separate in order to check the potential for arbitrary government. No such division is attempted in Europe and the roles of government are shared, rather than divided, amongst the institutions. It is not possible, therefore, to declare any single institution as the legislator, for example, of the EU.

The European Parliament (Arts 189–201 of the EC Treaty)

Composition and functions of the Parliament

The EP (or Assembly, as it was officially known prior to the SEA) was created under the ECSC Treaty in 1952. It consisted of 78 members who were delegates of their own national parliaments, representing political, rather than national affiliations. While the role of a parliament traditionally involves a substantial legislative function, in this regard, the EP was initially limited to an advisory role, providing little more than a forum for debate.

Today, the EP is composed of 626 members (known as Members of the European Parliament or MEPs) who, since 1979, have been directly elected via democratic elections held every five years in each Member State. It is the largest multinational parliament in the world, *representing the interests* of approximately 400 m EU *citizens*. It sits in Strasbourg for monthly plenary sessions and holds committee meetings and additional sessions in Brussels, while its General Secretariat is based in Luxembourg. All of the EU's major political parties are represented and MEPs are grouped together according to their political affiliations, rather than by nationality.

The work of the EP, much of it done through committees, can be divided into three main areas:

- legislative;
- budgetary;
- supervisory.

Each of these powers will be considered in turn.

(i)   The legislative role of the European Parliament:

The legislative processes of the EC are complicated and can involve the participation of three of the EC's institutions: the Commission, whose role is largely to propose draft legislation; the Council, which must normally provide assent, and the Parliament, whose role varies depending on the *subject matter* of the proposed legislation. It is important to understand that not only are there different forms of EC legislation (most importantly, Regulations, Directives and Decisions), but also that there are, in total, six different processes by which legislation may be enacted.

Consultation

As already touched upon, the Parliament was originally provided with a purely consultative role with regard to the creation of European legislation. In order to distinguish this process from other legislative procedures, it has become known as the *'consultation procedure'*. This procedure requires that, before legislation may be adopted, the EP must be consulted. While neither the Council nor the Commission is required to act on any opinions or proposals for change put forward by the EP, failure to consult can lead to legislation being declared void by the ECJ (see, for example, Case 138/79, *Roquette Freres v Council*). The procedure is now less frequently used, having been superseded by new procedures that have strengthened Parliament's legislative powers.

Co-operation

Consideration of the ECSC Treaty demonstrates that, from the outset, it had been intended that the EP should eventually become elected by universal suffrage. It was not until 1974, however, in a meeting of the European Council, that it was decided that such elections should take place as 'soon as possible'. As a corollary to this, it was added that the powers of the Parliament should be extended, particularly with regard to the Community's legislative process. Direct elections have, without a doubt, given the EP greater legitimacy and authority and, as a result of calls for increased powers for the EP, the SEA introduced a new procedure to be known as *'co-operation'*. This is seen as being a first step in the extension of the powers of the democratically elected Parliament. Under this rather complicated new procedure, the EP may reject draft legislation which the Council may only subsequently adopt by unanimity, rather than the more usual qualified majority voting (QMV).

While by no means placing the EP on an equal footing with the Council in the legislative process, the new procedure increased Parliament's influence, resulting in both the Council and the Commission becoming more inclined to take on board the EP's points of view. Indeed, there is evidence to suggest that amendments proposed by Parliament were now far more likely to be adopted by the Commission and the Council. It should be remembered, however, that, at this stage, the consultation procedure was still very much the norm and that the new co-operation procedure was limited in its application to certain, rather narrow, areas.

Assent

In addition, the SEA also introduced a procedure known as the *'assent procedure'*, giving the EP the right of veto with regard to decisions of a *non-routine* legislative nature. In areas such as the accession of new Member States and agreements with non-Member States, the EP must provide its agreement before the Council can adopt a draft proposal. The TEU has since made some changes to this procedure and also extended it to, for example, all international agreements.

Co-decision

The TEU further increased the EP's legislative powers by introducing a procedure known as the *'co-decision'*. The main difference between the co-decision and co-operation procedures is that the former allows the EP to veto, by absolute majority, a proposed legislative measure. The importance of the procedure from the Parliament's point of view was that it allows the EP to prevent the Council from passing legislation without its agreement. It is important, however, to understand that Parliament was *not* given the power to enact legislation and, indeed, the use of the co-decision was limited, the co-operation procedure becoming the norm under the TEU. The ToA has since extended the use of co-decision, once more in effect increasing the influence of the EP in the Community's legislative process.

(ii)   The Parliament's budgetary role

Initially, the EP had, in line with its legislative powers, a purely consultative role in relation to the Community's budget. In 1970, major changes were made with regard to the funding of the Communities and this coincided with the first major extension of the EP's powers via the 1970 and 1975 Budgetary Treaties.

Four institutions have a part to play in the Community's budgetary procedures. The Commission is responsible for drawing up a draft budget the Council and Parliament adopt, while the CoA provides an annual audit. A draft budget will contain details of proposed compulsory and non-compulsory expenditure and also an estimate of revenue. The Parliament has the power to *amend* the sections of the budget relating to *non-compulsory* expenditure, but may only *suggest* amendments with regard to *compulsory* expenditure, as the Council has the last word in this area. Parliament does however, have the power to reject a draft budget in its entirety and has indeed done so on a number of occasions. When this happens, the Community must proceed on the basis of the previous year's budget until agreement can be reached.

The EP's budgetary role can therefore be described as substantial, but should not be over-estimated as, first, the largest share of the budget is compulsory and therefore largely controlled by the Council and, secondly, the EP has no control over revenue raising.

(iii) The Parliament's supervisory role

In the UK, an attempt is made to separate the various roles of government in order to prevent the centralisation of power. As there is no separation of powers within the EC, the EC Treaty provides for a number of 'checks and balances' to ensure that no one institution can become too powerful. As part of this system of checks and balances, the institutions all play a part in supervising each another.

Parliament and the Commission

One of the more important supervisory powers held by the EP is that which it has over the Commission. Under the ECSC Treaty, the Parliament (then the Assembly) was entitled to debate the annual report produced by the Commission (then the High Authority). Provided a two-thirds majority could be achieved, the EP could pass a motion of censure, requiring the Commission to resign *en bloc*. This power is still enjoyed by the Parliament but, to date, has never been used, probably because it has been seen as far too severe a sanction to impose and, also, in most circumstances, the EP and Commission consider themselves allies rather than adversaries. Also, until amendments were introduced by the TEU, the EP was unable to exert control over the appointment of new Commissioners and it would, therefore, have been rather pointless to sack the Commission when it had no control over who was to replace the outgoing Commissioners.

Parliament and the Council

The ECSC Treaty also provided that the EP may require the Commission to reply to oral or written questions put by them. In 1973, the Parliament made time in its schedule for a regular 'question time' with regard to *both* the Commission and the Council. While this power may be effective as a means of exposing wrongdoing, the Council, unlike the Commission, cannot be forced to reply to Parliament's questioning and neither is there any sanction available against them.

The Parliamentary ombudsman and maladministration

The European Parliament may also set up committees of inquiry to investigate allegations of maladministration. The TEU also provided that the EP may appoint an Ombudsman to receive complaints regarding possible maladministration against any EU body, received either directly from citizens or via an MEP. In addition, the Ombudsman may initiate inquiries on his own initiative. At the conclusion of an investigation, the Ombudsman is required to report to the EP, who have no powers to correct the situation but the process allows such maladministration to be brought to the attention of the media.

Parliament and judicial review

The EP may exert supervisory powers over the law making powers of the other institutions by instituting a legal challenge before the ECJ. This procedure, known as judicial review (which is discussed in further detail in Chapter 6), provides that the Parliament may, in appropriate circumstances as provided under Art 230 of the EC Treaty, challenge *legally effective acts* (largely secondary legislation) produced the Council, Commission or European Central Bank (ECB). It may, similarly, under Art 232 of the EC Treaty, challenge these institutions should they *fail to act* when bound to do so by Community rules. While it has always been clear that the EP may challenge another institution's failure to act, it was originally thought that the Parliament lacked *locus standi* to challenge an action under Art 230 of the EC Treaty (see Case 302/87, *European Parliament v Council*, the *Comitology* case). However, in the later *Chernobyl* case (Case C-70/88, *European Parliament v Council*), the ECJ declared that the Parliament might bring such an action in circumstances where it was trying to protect its rights or privileges. The EC Treaty has since been amended by the SEA, which formally acknowledged this right, and Parliament's role is now comparable, if not equal, to that of the Commission and the Council.

It can be concluded that the various powers of the Parliament, although initially weak, have substantially increased over time, largely as a result of their being directly and democratically elected. It can be argued that this is only right and proper, as it is the EP who enjoy the mandate of the peoples of Europe and to continue to deny Parliament a proper voice in Europe would have been to ignore the concept of democracy.

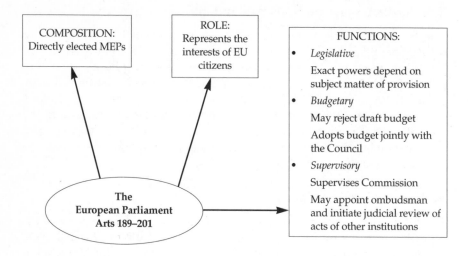

The Council of the European Union (Arts 202–10 of the EC Treaty)

The composition of the Council

The Council of Ministers or, as it has been formally known since the TEU, the Council of the European Union, is comprised of representatives (normally government ministers) from Member States authorised to *bind* the Government of that Member State. The composition of the Council at any one time will depend on the *subject matter* under discussion: for example, if the Council is discussing matters relating to agriculture, each Member State's agriculture minister will be present. Similarly, if transport matters are under discussion, transport ministers will attend.

The Council is led by a President. The Presidency of the Council rotates between the Member States on a six-monthly basis and it is the Member State holding the Presidency that decides what will be discussed and when.

The Committee of Permanent Representatives (COREPER)

Council ministers are supported by Permanent Representatives of the Member States (known collectively as COREPER, or the Committee of Permanent Representatives). COREPER consists of senior diplomats and it is instructive to note that it has been suggested that 90% of all EU decisions are actually taken by COREPER *before* they even reach ministerial level!

In addition to COREPER, the Council also has a General Secretariat providing administrative support.

The role of the Council

The Council represents national interests and, as a body, it has characteristics of both a supranational and intergovernmental organisation. The ministers who form the Council are responsible to their national parliaments, yet they form part of the institutional body that makes decisions on behalf of Europe. The EC Treaty provides that the function of the Council is to *'ensure that the objectives set out in the Treaty are attained'*.

The Council's legislative role

Originally, the Council was considered to be the principle *legislator* for the Community. Since developments wrought by the SEA, TEU and ToA, it now shares this role, although not equally, with the Parliament, with whom it also shares its budgetary powers (discussed above).

The Council's legislative powers can be summarised thus:

- the right to approve draft legislation placed before it by the Commission after the proper involvement of the European Parliament;
- the right (under Art 208 of the EC Treaty) to request that the Commission undertakes various studies and, as a result, submits proposals;
- the right to delegate legislative power to the Commission in areas where specific or detailed rules are required.

Reaching agreement in Council

In addition to its legislative powers, the Council sets political objectives, co-ordinates national policies and provides a forum where differences between Member States may be resolved. When the Council is required to reach a decision, it does so by taking a vote. There are three systems of voting that may be used by the Council: *simple majority, qualified majority* and *unanimity*. Reaching a decision by simple majority simply requires that the majority of Council ministers support a proposal for it to be passed. This requires Member States to surrender a high degree of sovereignty and, therefore, is rarely used.

Initially, the favoured method of voting was unanimity, effectively allowing each Member State the power of veto. While this method is still used, especially with regard to constitutional matters, qualified majority voting (QMV) has become a regular feature of Council lawmaking, particularly since amendments introduced by the SEA increased its use. Under this method, each Member State's vote is 'weighted' to reflect the size of its population (see Art 205 of the EC Treaty). Out of a possible total of 87 votes, in order for a measure to be adopted, there must be a minimum of 62 in favour. This method of reaching decisions means that a Member State may find itself bound by a decision which it does not approve of.

The Luxembourg Accords

When, in 1966, the Council moved towards the regular use of QMV, France refused to attend Council meetings (known as the 'empty chair' policy), objecting to the resulting loss of sovereignty. This protest resulted in what has become known as the Luxembourg Compromise (or Accords), when it was agreed that, should a decision be required on an issue relating to 'very important interests' of a Member State, that State would be treated as having a right of veto. This had the effect of increasing the power of the Council, who represent Member State interests, and decreasing the influence of the Commission, who represent the interests of the Community as a whole. The effect of this 'veto' should not be over-emphasised, however, as, before it may be evoked, a Member State must successfully

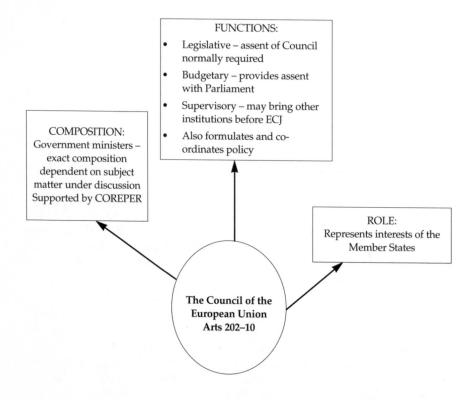

demonstrate that the issue in question relates to sufficiently important interests and it is seen very much as a measure of last resort.

The European Council

Take care not to confuse the European Council with either the Council of Ministers (or as it is now known, the Council of the European Union) or the Council of Europe (which is outside both the EC and the EU – see Chapter 2).

The European Council is composed of the Heads of *Government or State* of the Member States. Regular meetings (known as summits) have been taking place between such heads since the 1960s, but the decision to formalise such meetings was not taken until 1974. While Member States' interests were already represented in the Council of Ministers (as discussed above), it was apparently concluded that strategy for the development of the Community should be concluded at the highest possible political level. In addition, it was seen as an appropriate forum for settling disagreements of fundamental importance between Member States.

Despite its rather uncertain institutional status, the European Council has become increasingly important, providing political direction and the impetus for development within Europe. Major changes to the Treaties are, for example, preceded by summit meetings which, in turn, will lead on to an intergovernmental conference (IGC) from which amendments to primary legislation will emerge.

It was agreement at European Council level that led to the introduction of direct elections for the European Parliament and also to the creation of a European unit of currency, while the impetus for the European Union was a result of an *ad hoc* committee set up by the European Council (The Dooge Committee). Other topics regularly debated by the European Council include the state of the European economy and external relations.

The European Council has regular contact with other institutions: its membership includes the President of the Commission, while the President of the European Parliament is often invited to attend and reports are regularly submitted to the EP on any progress being achieved.

The European Council can be seen as an example of the way in which the Community has evolved. While its beginnings can be traced back to a series of *ad hoc* meetings, it is now recognised and valued as an important decision making body.

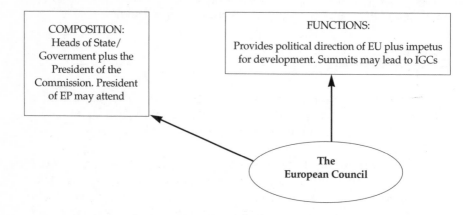

The European Commission (Arts 211–13 of the EC Treaty)

The Commission's position within the institutional balance of the Community has varied considerably during its lifetime, fluctuating between being heralded as the embryonic European government and the Community's civil service. The Commission's position within the institutional balance has undoubtedly suffered as a result of the increased power enjoyed by the EP and the 'Brussels bureaucrats' are seen to be held in low esteem by the general public – at least if the UK's popular press are to be believed. Publicity surrounding the Commission's *en bloc* resignation in 1999 as a result of allegations of malpractice did little to improve its reputation, despite its commitment to 'transparency' in the exercise of its functions. On the whole, however, the Commission can be seen as a success, as the progress made with regards to European integration could not have been achieved without the Institution's input as motivator, monitor and negotiator.

The composition of the Commission

The Commission is comprised of 20 Commissioners; by convention, two from each of the larger Member States and one from each of the others. (When the proposed enlargement of the Community takes place, the ToA has provided that the number of Commissioners will remain unchanged, requiring that the larger Member States relinquish their 'extra' Commissioner.)

Commissioners, who must be EC citizens, are nominated by the governments of the Member States, subject to the approval of the European Parliament. The EC Treaty requires that each Commissioner be independent and Commissioners are required to swear an oath promising not to take instruction from any government or other body, and to act only in the interests of the Community. (There has, however, been some debate over their impartiality as Commissioners who find themselves 'out of tune' with the government of their Member State may find that they are not re-appointed.) While a Commissioner, who fails to fulfil the conditions of his appointment, may be dismissed by the ECJ, the EP may also dismiss the Commission *en bloc*, as discussed above. (It is relevant to note that the involvement of the EP in the appointment of the Commission is considered to be a positive step, thereby increasing its democratic legitimacy.)

The governments of the Member States also appoint a President from amongst the Commissioners, after first consulting the EP. This is a particularly influential post, as the President will not only chair Commission meetings and attend the meetings of the European Council but also represent Europe at international summits. The Commission is divided into 25 directorates-general (DGs), each headed by a director-general who in turn reports to a Commissioner with overall responsibility for the work of that DG. Numbered from I to XXIV, DGs are divided by subject matter, for example, DGIII relates to Industry while DGXXII deals with matters relating to Education, Training and Youth. Each Commissioner is supported by a cabinet and the Commission has a total staff of approximately 18,000.

The role of the Commission

While the European Parliament represent the interests of the citizens of Europe and the Council the interests of the Member States, the Commission represents the interests of the Community as a whole. Article 211 of the EC Treaty provides that the Commission must *'ensure the proper functioning and development of the common market'* and this has resulted in the Commission becoming known as the *'Guardian of the Treaties'*.

The Commission is a multi-purpose organisation and its functions include the legislative, administrative, executive and quasi-judicial as outlined below.

(i)   The Commission's legislative role

The Commission plays a central role in the Community's legislative process, its most important function being that of *initiator* of draft legislation. As has already been discussed above in relation to the EP, the Commission will produce draft legislation which it then sends to the Council and the EP for their consideration and/or approval. The Commission further participates in the legislative process by amending legislative proposals in circumstances where either the Council or Parliament (or both) have failed to provide the necessary agreement, often reacting to amendments suggested by those institutions.

Many of the Commission's proposals for legislation are a direct result of Council requests that various studies be undertaken (under Art 208 of the EC Treaty) and, since amendments introduced by the TEU, the EP may also request that the Commission submit legislative proposals on appropriate matters (Art 192 of the EC Treaty). The Commission now publishes an annual programme outlining its legislative plans and listing legislative priorities for that year, thereby playing a part in planning the strategy for the Community as a whole. In addition, the Commission has been dubbed the 'motor for integration' of the Community, due to its involvement in the development of policy. This can be evidenced by the Commission's White Paper entitled *Completion of the Internal Market* (COM (85)310), which was significant in the shaping of the SEA.

The Commission also has the power, in very limited circumstances, to act alone in the making of EC legislation. (This can be evidenced by reference to Art 86(3) of the EC Treaty.) In addition, the Council may delegate legislative powers to the Commission, once more in limited circumstances.

(ii)   The Commission's administrative and executive roles

Legislation, once enacted, must be implemented and policy, once made, must be put into effect. The Commission's role is generally not one of direct action, as both policy and legislation are largely put into effect at national level, but the Commission maintains a supervisory position, ensuring that the appropriate Member States' agencies comply.

The Commission manages the EU's annual budget, including a number of funds such as the European Social Fund and, importantly, the European Agricultural and Guarantee Fund which takes up approximately 50% of the Community's annual budget.

The Commission also has a central role with regard to the Community's external relations. The EU's effectiveness on a global level is enhanced by the Commission's role as negotiator of trade and co-operation agreements with countries or groups of countries outside the Community. The Commission, for example, represents the EU at the United Nations and its specialised agencies such as the World Trade Organisation (see Art 302 of the EC Treaty).

(iii)   The Commission's quasi-judicial function

The Commission has two separate judicial (or quasi-judicial) functions. First, Art 226 of the EC Treaty provides the Commission with the power to investigate, and bring before the ECJ, any Member State that it considers to be in breach of Community obligations. The Commission attempts to remedy any breach as informally as possible, through consultation and negotiation with the errant Member State and an action before the ECJ is seen very much as a last resort. (This action is discussed in further detail in Chapter 6.)

Secondly, the Commission plays an important role in ensuring that Community rules relating to competition are followed. For example, any undertaking (the favoured EC term for a firm or individual capable of economic activity) that attempts to distort trade within the Community may find itself in breach of Community law (notably Arts 81 and 82 of the EC Treaty). Under *Regulation 17* (1956–62 OJ Spec Ed 87), the Commission is provided with the power to investigate possible breaches, provide formal decisions as to whether there has been an infringement and impose fines against any wrongdoers. While the investigative and forensic powers of the Commission may be subject to judicial review, these functions provide the Commission with significant influence in relation to the development of EC policy.

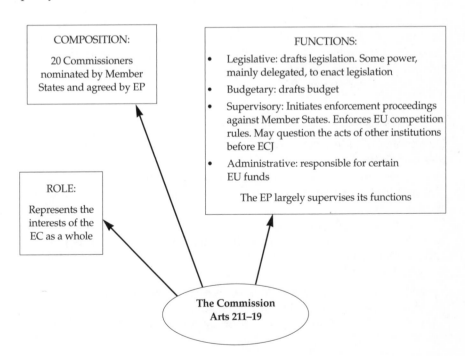

COMPOSITION:

20 Commissioners nominated by Member States and agreed by EP

FUNCTIONS:

- Legislative: drafts legislation. Some power, mainly delegated, to enact legislation
- Budgetary: drafts budget
- Supervisory: Initiates enforcement proceedings against Member States. Enforces EU competition rules. May question the acts of other institutions before ECJ
- Administrative: responsible for certain EU funds

    The EP largely supervises its functions

ROLE:

Represents the interests of the EC as a whole

The Commission
Arts 211–19

In can be concluded that the Commission's functions elevate it far above that of a 'civil service' for the Community. It can be described as a *sui generis*, multi-functional organisation with not inconsiderable influence over not only the day to day running of the Community, but also its development and direction. This said, its powers are not boundless and many are held under the discretion of the Council and the supervision of the EP.

The European Court of Justice (Arts 220–45 of the EC Treaty)

The European Communities are founded on the rule of law and acceptance by the Member States, institutions and individuals of the binding nature of its 'rules' is fundamental to the EC's existence. The role of the ECJ is to ensure that, in the interpretation and application of the Treaty, the law is observed (Art 220 of the EC Treaty). Since November 1989, the Court of First Instance (CFI) has assisted the ECJ in its task. Both the ECJ and the CFI sit in Luxembourg.

The composition and structure of the ECJ

The ECJ is made up of a number of personnel including *judges* and *Advocates General* (AGs). While the judges act as the decision makers of the Court, AGs, who have no equivalent in the UK's legal system, assist the judges by delivering a non-binding written opinion, which provides advice to the Court prior to their deliberations.

(i)   Judges

The number of judges composing the Court is dependent on the number of Member States. At present, there are 15 Member States and, consequently, the Court is made up of 15 judges. Should there be an even number of Member States, an additional judge is selected from one of the larger Member States, ensuring that there is always an uneven number of judges. The appointment of judges is '*by common accord of the governments of the Member States*' (Art 223 of the EC Treaty) and re-appointment is possible and, in fact, common. Judges enjoy a six year term of office, which is staggered to avoid all the judges being replaced at the same time.

The Treaty requires that judges be '*persons whose independence is beyond doubt*' and it is clear that judges must be independent of any government or interest group. As with all fixed term appointments, it is possible that political pressure could be brought to bear on judges. This is reduced however as the Court's deliberations are secret, with a *single* ruling being delivered by the Court rather than individual judgments.

With regard to the qualifications that must be held by a judge of the ECJ, the Treaty requires that they must *'possess the qualifications required for appointment to the highest judicial offices in their respective countries or who are jurisconsults of recognised competence'*. While the UK has so far chosen to appoint domestic judges or legal practitioners, the Treaty allows academics to be appointed and a number of other EC States have done so.

The Court appoints a President, who directs the work of the Court, from amongst its judges and also a Registrar.

(ii)   Advocates General

In addition to the judges, the ECJ also has eight Advocates General. Once more the number is dependent on the number of Member States, with five being appointed from the larger States while the others are appointed on rota basis from amongst the remaining States. The rules relating to the appointment and qualifications of the AGs are the same as those for judges.

The role of the ECJ

The Treaty provides the Court's jurisdiction. The various actions that can be brought before the Court can be divided into *direct* actions and *preliminary rulings*. Direct actions include those brought by the Commission against Members States accused of failing to fulfil their Community obligations and actions brought by the Institutions or individuals wishing to challenge the validity of Community legislation (both are discussed in further detail in Chapter 6).

Preliminary rulings, on the other hand, are the result of requests by national courts requiring the ECJ to either *interpret* EC law or rule on the *validity* of EC secondary legislation. National courts will make such requests when they have a case before them that revolves on a point of Community law (see Chapter 6).

In addition to its specific jurisdiction, the Treaty provides that the Court has the rather general function of ensuring the *'law is observed'*.

It has been argued that the ECJ has used this rather broad remit to expand its role beyond that normally performed by a judicial body. The ECJ has adopted a purposive, teleological or contextual, rather than literal, approach to interpreting EC law. As it explained in Case 283/81, *CILFIT*:

'*Every provision of Community law must be placed in its context and interpreted in the light of the provisions of Community law as a whole, regard being given to the objectives thereof.*' This has allowed the Court to take a major role in filling gaps left by Community legislation which, in turn, has resulted in its being accused of usurping the role of both the Community legislators and policy makers.

Such activism has been denied by both the Court and its supporters, who argue that the ECJ has gone no further than was necessary, given the nature of the Treaty, which is intended to be no more than a framework.

It cannot be denied that the Court has produced some particularly dynamic decisions and one has to look no further than Case 26/62, *Van Gend en Loos*, to see the impact that the Court has had on the development of EC law (see Chapter 5). It has been argued, however, that the ECJ is now playing a far less proactive role, perhaps now content that the Treaty has been sufficiently constitutionalised and the legal order adequately developed. Whether this is so or not will only be clear in hindsight.

Procedure before the ECJ

Procedure before the Court can be divided into two stages – oral and written. Unlike the UK however, emphasis is placed on written submissions, while the oral stage is limited and short (which is probably advantageous, as the case may be heard in any of the Community's 11 official languages).

The written stage comes first, with relevant documents being communicated to all parties. At the end of the written stage cases may be argued orally in open court and it is following this hearing that the AG will deliver his opinion.

The judges, who may sit in plenary session (minimum of seven judges) or in chambers of three or five judges, deliberate behind closed doors, delivering their judgment in open court. The judgment, which will be made available in all 11 official languages, will include the reasoning on which it is based. (It is worth noting that the AG's opinion is often more readable than the ECJ's judgment and is, therefore, generally worth examining.)

The Court of First Instance

The CFI, which consists of 15 judges, was established under the SEA as a means of relieving the excessive workload of the ECJ. The jurisdiction of the Court is limited to actions brought by natural and legal individuals and there is a right of appeal to the ECJ on points of law.

While the creation of a CFI has undoubtedly removed some of the burden from the ECJ, there are still calls to rethink the structure of the ECJ, particularly in the light of EU enlargement. It had been widely expected that the ToA would have introduced reforms to the Court's structure and organisation, but this was not the case other than *extending* its jurisdiction to new matters under the reformed Pillar III.

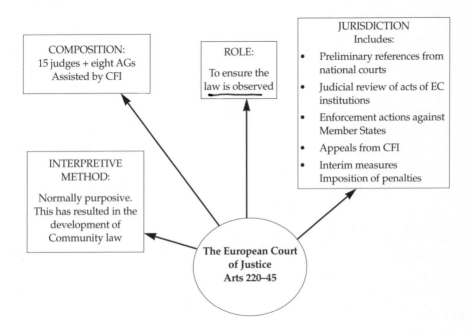

The Court of Auditors (Arts 246–48 of the EC Treaty)

The Court was established by the Budgetary Treaty 1975, but it was not until the TEU came into effect that it was afforded the status of Community institution. It is comprised of 15 members, one from each Member State. Both the Council and EP are involved in the appointment procedure and auditors must be appropriately qualified and their independence beyond doubt.

While the Court of Auditors (CoA) has been afforded the title of 'court', its function is not judicial. It is rather the taxpayer's representative, a 'watchdog' over the EU's money and as the Union's budget has increased, so has the prominence of the Court – although it still remains 'low-key' compared to the other four institutions. Every institution and body that has access to Union funds is subject to the scrutiny of the CoA and the Court provides a check that all legal requirements are observed and also that the Community is receiving value for money.

The CoA publishes an annual report, highlighting any areas where improvements are possible or desirable. The Court also provides the EP and the Council with a Statement of Assurance, which declares that EU money has been spent for the purposes intended.

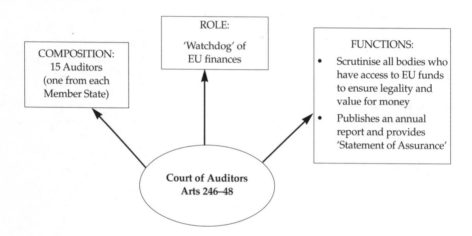

Other Community bodies

The EC Treaty also makes provision for ECOSOC and a Committee of Regions (CoR) (Art 7 of the EC Treaty), a European System of Central Banks (ESCB) as well as the ECB (Art 8 of the EC Treaty) and, also, a European Investment Bank (EIB) (Art 9 of the EC Treaty). Each of these will be considered, briefly, in turn.

The Economic and Social Committee

The ECOSOC is a consultative body, which represents a variety of sectional interests. Its membership consists of 222 representatives drawn from a broad cross-section of society such as workers, employees, farmers, craftsmen, professionals, consumer groups, etc. Meetings are held on a monthly basis.

The EC Treaty requires that draft legislation, in specific policy areas, be referred to the Committee and the majority of new EC laws of any significance have been adopted only following input from ECOSOC.

The Committee of Regions

The youngest of the EU's institutions, the CoR was established by the TEU to represent regional and local interests. Like the ECOSOC, it has a membership of 222, drawn from around the Member States, and must be consulted by the Council and Commission where the EC Treaty so specifies.

As national barriers break down and borders between the Member States become more open as a consequence of the EC's single market, the creation of a Committee of regions can be seen as a response to peoples fears over centralisation. The CoR has direct experience of how EU policies affect the everyday life of citizens and their expertise allows them to bring a powerful influence to bear.

The European System of Central Banks and the European Central Bank

The TEU provided a legal basis for Economic and Monetary Union (EMU) and, as part of the third stage of EMU, the ESCB and ECB were created with the primary aim of maintaining price stability (Art 105 of the EC Treaty). The ESCB is composed of the ECB and the national central banks of Member States participating in monetary union. The Treaty provides that *'the ESCB shall support the general economic policies in the Community'*, providing this does not conflict with the pursuit of price stability.

European Investment Bank

The EIB, whose membership comprises the 15 Member States, is the EU's financing institution, providing long term loans for capital investments which promote the Community's economic development and integration. It supports regional development and its loans are often accompanied by grants from the EU's Structural and Cohesion Funds.

CONCLUSIONS

So, who runs Europe? The answer, of course, depends on what is meant by 'run' and, to some extent, what is meant by 'Europe'. We have already seen that when we are talking about the 'running' of the European Communities (Pillar I), the main actors differ from those who 'run' the other two Pillars that make up the EU, with the various roles undertaken by the institutions varying considerably.

However, when we consider who wields power and influence in Europe we need to consider more than just the Institutions and the Governments of the Member States and also consider regional authorities. It has been argued that the day of the nation State is over as Member States are allegedly too small to run international affairs or compete effectively in world markets.

Conversely, it has also been argued that the Brussels bureaucracy is too far removed from everyday life – hence the emerging importance of regional authorities within the Community. The principle of subsidiary found under Art 3b of the EC Treaty, appears to support the sharing of responsibility amongst the various levels of authority.

It can be concluded therefore, that while the European Council is undoubtedly the most influential body in relation to policy making and direction, no one body has absolute control within Europe. Instead, it is run on the basis of co-operation and negotiation between a variety of authorities.

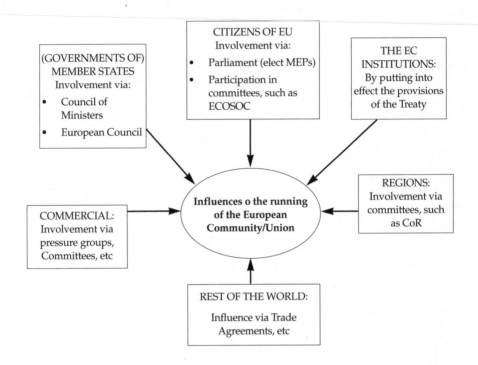

4 Community Law

In order to develop an understanding of European law, its sources need to be examined. Community law can be divided into two categories, namely *primary* and *secondary*. The primary source of European Community (EC) law is the various *Treaties,* both those that were enacted in order to create the European Communities and, also, those that have been enacted in order to *amend* the original Treaties.

Secondary sources include *secondary legislation*, as enacted by the institutions of the Community, *case law*, which is derived from the judgments of the European Court of Justice (ECJ), *general principles*, as articulated by the ECJ and *international agreements* entered into by the Community. Each of these sources will be considered in turn.

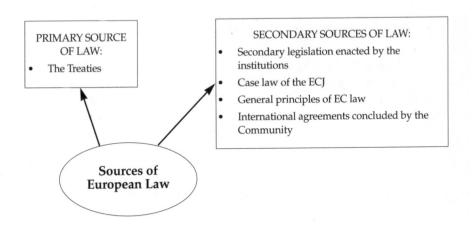

(1)   PRIMARY SOURCES OF EC LAW

As already touched upon, the principal sources of law for the European Communities are the Treaties that created those Communities, namely:

- the Treaty establishing the European Coal and Steel Community 1951 (also known as the Treaty of Paris or the ECSC Treaty);
- the Treaty establishing the European Atomic Energy Community 1957 (the First Treaty of Rome or the Euratom Treaty);
- the Treaty establishing the European Economic Community 1957 (also known as the Treaty of Rome and the EEC Treaty, but now known as the EC Treaty).

The most important Treaty from the point of the European Community is, of course, the last of these. There have also been a number of Treaties enacted which have amended this Treaty and these *include*:

- the Merger Treaty 1965;
- the Budgetary Treaties 1970 and 1975;
- the Single European Act (SEA) 1986;
- the Treaty on European Union (TEU) 1992 (also known as the Maastricht Treaty)*;
- the Treaty of Amsterdam (ToA) 1997.

* It should be noted that the TEU could be included in either list as, not only did it amend the EC Treaty, but also created the EU.

Creating primary legislation

The European Council has become pivotal to the initiation of any new Treaty. The process generally involves the Council concluding, at a summit meeting, that an intergovernmental conference (IGC) is needed in order to discuss any reforms that may prove necessary. For amendments to be agreed at an IGC there must be common accord by the representatives of the governments of the Member States. Once such agreement is reached each Member State, in accordance with its respective constitutional requirements, must then ratify any new treaty. Once such ratification is obtained, a date can be set for the implementation of the treaty.

SECONDARY SOURCES OF EC LAW

(i)   Secondary legislation

Article 249 of the EC Treaty provides that: '... the European Parliament acting jointly with the Council, the Council and the Commission shall make regulations and issue directives, take decisions, make recommendations and deliver opinions.'

From this Article, it is clear that three of the Community's Institutions may be concerned with the creation of secondary legislation and that there are five forms that such legislation may take. (The processes involved in creating secondary legislation will be considered later.)

Community legislators (usually the Commission) are free to choose which form legislation is to take *unless* the Treaty otherwise prescribes it. Each form of secondary legislation will be considered in turn.

Regulations

Article 249 of the EC Treaty provides that: 'A regulation shall have general application. It shall be binding in its entirety and directly applicable in all Member States.'

The fact that a regulation will have 'general application' and is 'binding in its entirety' simply means that a regulation will be effective throughout the Community, on *every* Member State and in *full*. Regulations must be published in the Official Journal and come into force on the date specified by the regulation or, if no such date is specified, on the 20th day following publication.

The exact meaning of 'direct applicability' has been the cause of some debate, but it is now accepted that it denotes that regulations *automatically* take effect in each Member State without the need for national adopting measures. The ECJ has gone as far as to provide that Member States shall not pass any measure which professes to incorporate a Community regulation in to national law (see, for example, Case 34/73, *Variola*), as this could result in each member State placing its own interpretation on the legislation.

Regulations achieve *uniformity of law* throughout the EC.

Directives

Article 249 of the EC Treaty provides that, 'a directive shall be binding, as to the result to be achieved, upon each Member State to which it is addressed, but shall leave to the national authorities the choice of form and methods'.

Directives differ from regulations in a number of ways. They do not have general application and so do not have to be addressed to *all* Member States. In addition, only directives that are addressed to all Member States and those which are created by means of the 'co-decision' procedure (which is discussed below), need be published in the Official Journal (Art 254 of the EC Treaty).

Directives are not directly applicable and, normally, the rights and obligations created by them only become effective once they have been incorporated into national law by the appropriate national authorities. They do, however, place an obligation on Member States to ensure that a particular aim is achieved by a particular date, leaving national authorities to decide on the implementation details. This allows a far greater degree of *flexibility*, providing Member States with the opportunity to introduce a measure in the manner best suited to that State.

Decisions are often the chosen method where *harmonisation*, rather than uniformity, of law is the aim.

Decisions

Article 249 of the EC Treaty provides that, 'a decision shall be binding in its entirety upon those to whom it is addressed'.

A decision is similar to a regulation in that it has direct applicability, requiring no national implementation in order to take effect. All decisions must be published in the Official Journal, taking effect at a prescribed time or on the 20th day following publication.

It should be noted however, that decisions are only binding upon those to *whom they are addressed*. (Decisions may be addressed to individual Member States and both natural and legal persons.)

Recommendations and opinions and 'soft' law

Unlike regulations, directives and decisions, recommendations and opinions are *not legally binding*.

Article 249 of the EC Treaty provides that they have *'no binding force'*, although they are *persuasive* and should be taken into account by national courts (see Case C–322/88, *Grimaldi*). Such sources of law are sometimes known as *'soft law'*. Other sources of soft law may include guidelines or codes of conduct issued by the Community Institutions.

Creating secondary legislation

All binding Community secondary legislation is subject to review by the ECJ which may adjudicate on its validity. It is particularly important that the correct procedures are followed when creating such legislation, as failure to do so may render the legislation invalid. (Judicial review of legally enforceable acts of the institutions is discussed in Chapter 6.)

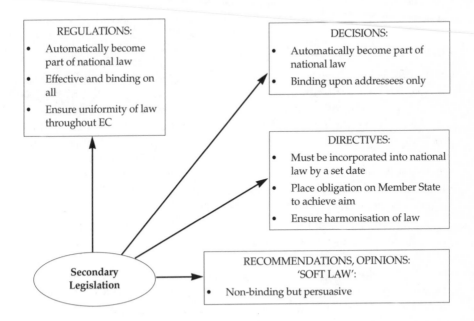

REGULATIONS:
• Automatically become part of national law
• Effective and binding on all
• Ensure uniformity of law throughout EC

DECISIONS:
• Automatically become part of national law
• Binding upon addressees only

DIRECTIVES:
• Must be incorporated into national law by a set date
• Place obligation on Member State to achieve aim
• Ensure harmonisation of law

Secondary Legislation

RECOMMENDATIONS, OPINIONS: 'SOFT LAW':
• Non-binding but persuasive

The legal base for the creation of secondary legislation

Community legislators must demonstrate that they have the necessary *authority* to enact secondary legislation. Article 253 of the EC Treaty provides that the preamble to regulations, directives and decisions should contain a statement as to the legal basis on which the legislation is made. Such authority will derive from a Treaty article empowering the institutions to legislate and is known as the 'legal base'.

The choice of legal base will depend on the *subject matter* of the proposed legislation. If, for example, the Community wish to legislate on the free movement of workers, the Community's legal 'authority' for doing so is provided by Art 40 of the EC Treaty. Where no specific law making powers are provided Art 308 of the EC Treaty may provide a *general power to legislate* in order to attain '*one of the objectives of the Community*'.

The Treaty article that provides the legal base for legislation will also specify which of the six legislative *procedures* should be followed.

Legislative procedures

The Community's legislative process is complicated, providing a total of *six* procedures by which secondary legislation may be enacted. Which procedure is to be followed in any one set of circumstances does *not* depend on the form that the legislation is to take but on the procedure identified by the *legal base*. Thus, for example, if the Community wish to enact legislation relating to the free movement of workers, the subject matter and therefore the legal base (Art 40 of the EC Treaty) will be the decisive feature *not* the form that the legislation was to take – the procedure would *not* differ if a directive were drafted rather than a regulation.

Generally, the Commission is the *initiator* of draft legislation. This can be at their own instigation or following a request from the Council (Art 208 of the EC Treaty) or the Parliament (Art 192 of the EC Treaty).

In most circumstances, the Council will be the *adopting* institution. The primary distinguishing feature of each procedure is the degree of involvement that it provides to the EP, although it may also have an effect on which method of voting must be followed by the Council – that is simple majority, unanimity or, more usually, qualified majority. (The implications of which voting procedure is applicable is discussed further, p 52, below.)

Outlines of the various procedures are provided below.

The Commission acting alone

This method is rarely used and it is sufficient to say that it involves the Commission acting without intervention from the other Community Institutions. (An example of the use of this procedure may be found under Art 86(3) of the EC Treaty.)

The Commission also enjoys delegated legislative power. Although not strictly a legislative procedure, the Council may, through parent legislation, authorise the Commission to enact regulations in specific areas such as agriculture and competition, this allows legislation to be enacted quickly in areas that are highly regulated.

The Council and Commission acting alone

Here the Council may adopt a proposal from the Commission without having to refer to any other authority. (An example of this procedure may be found under Art 26 of the EC Treaty.)

The 'consultation' procedure

Under this procedure the Commission puts forward a draft proposal to the Council, who, in turn, pass it to the EP for its opinion. No obligation is placed on either the Council or the Commission to follow such an opinion but the resulting legislation may be annulled if the EP is not consulted (see, for example, Case 138/79, *Roquette Freres v Council*).

This procedure was provided by the original Treaty and, therefore, before the EP became a directly elected body. It endows the EP with very little power, other than that of bringing the provision to the attention of others through debate. No longer the 'norm', it is still used in a number of areas, an example of which can be found under Art 19 of the EC Treaty.

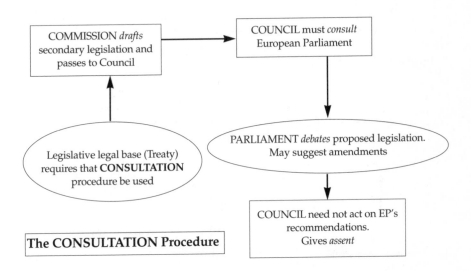

The 'co-operation' procedure

This procedure was established by the SEA in order to provide the EP with greater legislative powers, following the introduction of direct elections.

The procedure, which is contained within Art 252 of the EC Treaty, provides that the Council, following a proposal from the Commission, and on which it has obtained the EP's opinion, will adopt a 'common position', which, in turn, is communicated to the EP. The EP then has a number of avenues open to it. It may:

(a) *approve the common position* – in which case, the Council may adopt the proposal by qualified majority;

(b) *fail to reply* within three months – in which case, once more, the Council may adopt the provision as above;

(c) *reject common position* OR *propose amendments* – in which case, the Council may overrule the EP *but only if the Council acts unanimously.*

If unanimity is not possible, the Commission will be required to re-submit, within one month, the draft legislation after taking into account the EP's amendments. The Council may then adopt the proposal, normally within three months.

While this procedure clearly provides the EP with more legislative power than it enjoyed previously, it does not give the Parliament the power to enact or veto legislation. It was however considered to be a major innovation in the Community system requiring both the Council and Commission to take far more cognizance of the Parliament's opinions.

Since its introduction, the Community has continued to enhance the legislative powers of the EP via other legislative procedures and, as a result, the range of application of the co-operation procedure has significantly diminished.

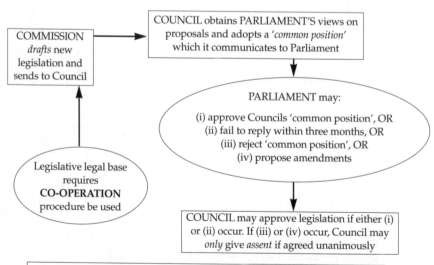

The CO-OPERATION Procedure: Art 252 of the EC Treaty

The 'co-decision' procedure

Introduced by the TEU, this procedure, provided by Art 251 of the EC Treaty, further enhances the powers of the EP.

Now modified by the ToA, this complex procedure initially involves the Commission sending a legislative proposal to both the Council and the EP. At this stage, providing agreement can be reached, the Council may adopt the legislation by qualified majority.

Should consensus not be reached, the Council may adopt a 'common position', which must be communicated to the EP. The EP has three months to approve the Council's common position. If approved, the legislation may be adopted. (Failure to reply within three months will have the same effect.) If, on the other hand, the EP *rejects*, by absolute majority, the Council's common position the proposed act will be deemed to have failed.

Alternatively, the EP may wish to propose amendments. Provided they do so after agreeing by absolute majority, such amendments should be sent to the Council and the Commission. Should the Council agree to the amendments within three months, the provision may be adopted by unanimity.

If agreement cannot be reached, a Conciliation Committee is set up, comprising representatives of both the Council and the EP and involving the Commission, in an attempt to reach consensus. There is then a period of

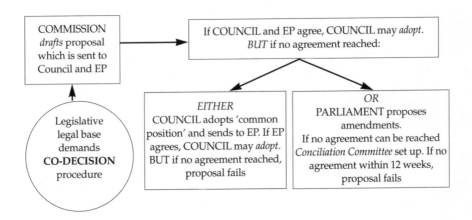

The CO-DECISION Procedure: Art 251 of the EC Treaty

12 weeks in which to agree and adopt the proposed legislation. It is possible that this period may be extended but if the text is not approved within the time limit set, it will be deemed not to have been adopted.

This procedure provides the EP with considerable legislative power as the Parliament may actually veto proposed legislation. This is particularly noteworthy, bearing in mind that each institution represents different, but equally important interests and goes some way in establishing the EP's position within the *institutional balance* of the Community.

The 'assent' procedure

In a small number of areas, the positive approval of the EP is required before the Council can adopt a proposal. This procedure, introduced by the SEA, affords the EP with an absolute power of rejection. An example of its use can be found under Art 161 of the EC Treaty.

Legislative processes – how decisions are reached

While it is important to get to grips with the variety of legislative procedures by which the Community may enact secondary legislation, there is far more to the legislative process than mere procedure.

The institutional balance

The original Treaty split power between the Council and the Commission and so, at the time, it was necessary to ensure the correct balance was reached between the federal tendencies of the Commission and the intergovernmental nature of the Council. The need to ensure balance within the Community has since been complicated by the introduction of direct elections to Parliament, which has consequently demanded, and received, far greater involvement in the legislative process.

As each of these institutions represent different interests (the Council, the Member States, the Parliament, the citizens and the Commission, the Community as a whole), the legislative processes have to ensure that all such interests are appropriately balanced.

Inter-institutional co-operation

As legislative procedures have developed there has been far greater need to ensure inter-institutional co-operation, both in the planning of legislative strategies and with regard to the content of legislative acts. With regard to the former, an inter-institutional co-ordination group (known as the Neuneither Group, after its founder) has, for example, been set up to plan future legislative programmes and the Commission consults widely with interested parties before putting forward legislative proposals.

Such consultation allows the interests of the Member States, citizens, the Community as a whole and variety of pressure groups to be taken into consideration.

In addition to co-operation between the institutions with regard to the formulation of legislative policies, with the increased use of the co-decision procedure in particular, there is also a need for inter-institutional co-operation in order to ensure policies become Acts.

Once the Commission has formulated draft legislation, it will be sent to the Parliament and/or the Council (depending on the procedure to be followed), which will consider the proposal, usually via a number of working groups or committees.

At this stage, there may be conflict between Member States within the Council or between political groups within the Parliament, and agreement will have to be reached within the institutions by means of negotiation and compromise. Once the Council and the Parliament have agreed their individual positions with regard to a legislative proposal, if their opinions diverge it will often be left to the Commission to broker agreement between the two if the legislative proposal is to succeed.

While the above discussion is, of necessity, brief, it hopefully provides some food for thought as to the democratic nature of the decision making processes within the Community. While the question of who runs Europe was considered in Chapter 3, it is suggested that issues are far more complex than they may first appear. Not only do the competing interests of the Community institutions have to be balanced, but also the competing interests of the various groups *within* the institutions, such as the various Member States, political parties, etc.

(2) CASE LAW OF THE EUROPEAN COURT OF JUSTICE

The Treaty of Rome gives the ECJ jurisdiction to hear various matters relating to the Community. The Court's prime function, as provided by Art 220 of the EC Treaty, is to *'ensure that in the interpretation and application of this Treaty the law is observed'* and, as the Treaties and secondary legislation are often imprecise or insufficiently comprehensive, this has provided the ECJ with the opportunity to contribute to the corpus of Community law.

The importance of the Court's decisions should not be underestimated, as the ECJ has developed far reaching principles such as the doctrines of *direct effect* and *supremacy* (see Chapter 5). By virtue of its purposive method of interpretation and with the aid of general principles of Community law (see below), the Court has filled gaps in the Treaties. (One of the more important functions of the Court, at least as far as their influence on EC law has been concerned, is that of the provision of *preliminary references* under Art 234 of the EC Treaty, which are also discussed in further detail in Chapter 5.)

While there is no formal system of precedent and the Court is free to depart from its own past decisions, in the interest of consistency, this seldom occurs. With regard to the relationship between the ECJ's decisions and national courts, the ECJ's decisions *do* have a precedential value as can be evidenced by the Court's *dicta* in Cases 28–30/62, *Da Costa*. (See Chapter 6.)

(3) GENERAL PRINCIPLES OF COMMUNITY LAW

General principles of law, which can be found in all advanced legal systems, have the function of assisting where written sources of law are not sufficiently comprehensive. The general principles of Community law have been developed by the ECJ and have been used to 'flesh out' the law found in the Treaties and secondary legislation.

General principles of Community law have been held to include:

- equality;
- fundamental human rights;
- proportionality;
- subsidiarity;
- legal certainty.

The function and status of general principles

General principles have been used by the ECJ to assist it in the interpretation of Community legislation and also as a factor when considering the validity of secondary legislation (see, for example, Case 112/77, *Topfer v Commission*). In addition, they provide a restraint on the activities of the Member States (for example, Case 11/70, *Internationale Handelsgesellschaft*, where the Court provided that a public authority must recognise the principle of proportionality in its dealings with citizens).

The ECJ has been creative in developing these principles, using the purposive method of interpretation and discovering them in:

- the Treaties;
- the legal systems of the Member States; and
- in international law.

The ECJ has justified its actions by referring to three Treaty Articles, which, it argues, give them the necessary authority, namely:

- Art 220 of the EC Treaty, which provides that: *'The Court of Justice shall ensure that in the interpretation of the Treaty the law is observed.'* The term 'law' in this context being understood to mean more than the written sources of law contained in the Treaties;

- Art 230 of the EC Treaty, which provides *'infringement of this Treaty or any rule of law relating to its application'*. 'Any rule of law' in this context has been interpreted to be a reference to law other than that contained in the Treaty;

- Art 288 of the EC Treaty, which refers to *'general principles common to the laws of the Member States'*.

In order to provide a flavour of how these principles have been developed and applied, a number of examples will be considered in turn.

Equality – discovered in the Treaties

The Treaty refers to the principle of equality on a number of occasions and is an example of the Court developing a general principle by bringing together 'threads' found in the Treaty.

While Art 12 of the EC Treaty prohibits discrimination on the grounds of nationality, Art 34(2) of the EC Treaty prohibits discrimination between producers or consumers within the Community. In addition, Art 141 of the EC Treaty provides for equal pay between men and women and the Court, on the basis of these 'threads', has developed a far more general principle of non-discrimination.

The Court has gone on to use the principle to prohibit discrimination based on grounds such as nationality (for example, Case 293/83, *Gravier v City of Liège*) and gender (for example, Cases 75a and 117/82, *Razzouk and Beydouin v Commission*).

The principle of equality or non-discrimination would now appear to be formally supported by the Treaty. Since the Treaty of Amsterdam came into force, Art 13 of the EC Treaty provides the Community with the authority to legislate in order to prohibit discrimination based on *'sex, racial or ethnic origin, religion or belief, disability, age or sexual orientation'*.

Fundamental human rights – discovered in national and international law

The ECJ, in cases such as Case 29/69, *Stauder v City of Ulm and Internationale Handelsgesellschaft*, has confirmed that rights guaranteed under German law are also to be protected by the Community.

Similarly, the ECJ, in Case 36/75, *Rutili v Ministre de l'Interieur*, confirmed that rights found in the Convention for the Protection of Human Rights and Freedoms (the ECHR) would be protected by Court.

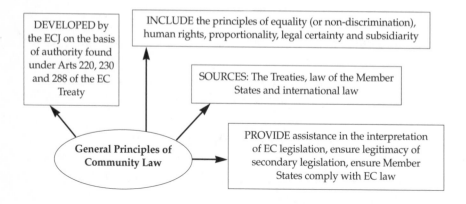

(4)   INTERNATIONAL AGREEMENTS

The EC (unlike the EU) has legal personality (see Art 281 of the EC Treaty) and is empowered (by Art 300 of the EC Treaty) to enter into international agreements which are an integral source of Community law.

The Commission has been provided with the role of negotiator of international agreements. Following authorisation by the Council, the Commission conducts negotiations, assisted by various committees. The Court may be required to consider the legality of any agreement, which will be put before the Council in the same manner as draft legislation. The Council may then give its assent to the agreement, after involving the European Parliament as appropriate to the field in which the agreement is being concluded (see Art 300 of the EC Treaty). Such agreements are binding on both the Community and on the Member States.

CONCLUSIONS

Community law is an evolving legal system, containing rules which provide rights, obligations and remedies. It has evolved over time and continues to develop in response to the needs and objectives of Europe. Contained in numerous sources, it is made up of rules which effectively provide the Community's constitution, direction on how the Community is to be administered and also the substantive law of the EC. Once this is understood, the time is right to consider the relationship that exists between Community law and the law of the Member States.

5 The Relationship Between Community Law and the Member States

THE DOCTRINES OF DIRECT EFFECT AND SUPREMACY

The status of European Community (EC) law within the legal systems of the various Member States is of fundamental importance and there are a number of questions that must be answered before an understanding of Community law can be gained.

First, it is necessary to consider the *effect* of EC law in the Member States, who receives rights and obligations under it and whether and where such rights may be enforced? Secondly, it is necessary to consider which 'level' of law will take precedence should there be any conflict between EC and national law.

Surprisingly, these questions were not addressed by the founding Treaties and it was assumed that EC law would have the same domestic effects as other sources of *international* law. This meant that the status of the EC Treaty in the Member States would be determined by each Member State's own constitutional rules.

In dualist States (such as the UK), international law is only binding on national courts if it has been adopted by the national authorities and made part of domestic law. On the other hand, in a monist State (such as the Netherlands), once ratified, international law automatically forms part of the national legal system.

In dualist States, it was therefore considered that the Treaties would not provide rights which could be invoked domestically by citizens *unless specifically incorporated* into national law, while, in Member States with monist constitutions, EC law automatically became part of that State's domestic legal system. In consequence, the status of EC law was thought to vary from State to State.

The European Court of Justice (ECJ) has, however, taken a different approach to the question of the impact of Community law and has developed two principles which have become known as the *'Twin Pillars'* upon which the Community rests, namely *direct effect* and *supremacy*. Each will be considered in turn.

(1) THE DOCTRINE OF DIRECT EFFECT OF EC LAW

The creation of the doctrine

The ECJ provided a ground breaking judgment in Case 26/62, *Van Gend en Loos* (*Van Gend*). *Van Gend en Loos* had imported a quantity of chemicals from Germany into the Netherlands and was required, by Dutch law, to pay customs duty to the Dutch authorities. The importers challenged the imposition of the duty in a Dutch tribunal, claiming that it was an infringement of Art 12 of the EC Treaty (now Art 25). The Dutch court referred the question to the ECJ under the preliminary reference procedure (Art 234 of the EC Treaty) (see Chapter 6).

In order to arrive at its decision, the ECJ drew heavily on its purposive method of interpretation, invoking not only the wording of the Treaties but also the spirit and aims of the Community. In its judgment, the ECJ declared that 'the Community constitutes a *new legal order* of international law' which confers both rights and obligations on individuals, as well as on the participating Member States, *without the need for implementing legislation*. The Court further concluded that national courts must protect such rights. In other words, the ECJ provided that EC law has direct effect, which can be seen as a two pronged concept under which:

(a) community law provides not only Member States with rights and obligations but individuals also; and

(b) such rights and obligations can be enforced by individuals before their national courts.

From this judgment, which was opposed by a number of Member States including the Netherlands and Belgium, it can be concluded that the Court was motivated by the need to ensure the *integration, effectiveness* and *uniformity* of Community law.

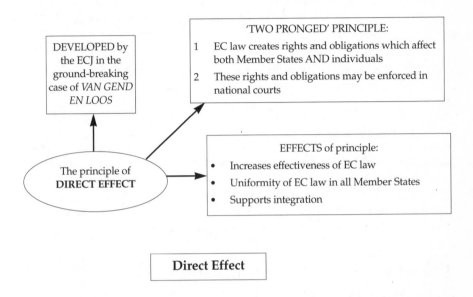

Direct Effect

The conditions for direct effect

The ECJ explained in *Van Gend* that not all Treaty articles would be capable of direct effect and it is now clear that a provision must fulfil a set of criteria (which will hereafter be called the *Van Gend* criteria for ease of explanation) if it is to have direct effect. The *Van Gend* criteria require that the legal provision must be as follows.

Clear

It is logical that if law is to be enforceable, both parties must be clear as to what their respective rights/obligations are. The ECJ have therefore declared that a provision must be 'sufficiently precise' before being capable of direct effect. This does not necessarily mean that the whole provision must comply: in Case 43/75, *Defrenne v Sabena*, for example, it was held that only part of Art 119 of the EC Treaty (now Art 141) fulfilled this criteria and was consequently directly effective.

Unconditional

A provision will not be unconditional if the right it provides is in some way dependant on the judgment or discretion of an independent body *unless* that discretion is subject to judicial control (see, for example, Case 41/74, *Van Duyn*).

Not subject to any further implementing measures on the part of either the Community or national authority

This criterion would appear to have been subject to rather liberal application by the ECJ, as can be demonstrated in Case 2/74, *Reyners v Belgium*. In this case, based on the wording of the Treaty, it had been anticipated that the Community would have to enact secondary legislation before the objectives contained in Art 52 of the EC Treaty (now Art 43) would provide rights to individuals. The Court however declared the provision directly effective, explaining that to do otherwise could result in individuals being denied their Community law rights.

Direct effect of the various sources of Community law

The doctrine of direct effect has been developed and expanded upon over the years and one important development has been with regard to the *sources* of EC law that may be directly effective.

(i) Direct effect and Treaty Articles

As we have already seen above, the question of whether the principle of direct effect applies to Treaty articles was considered in the ground-breaking judgment of *Van Gend en Loos* when Art 12 of the EC Treaty (now Art 25) was held to have direct effect. It is now accepted that Treaty articles are capable of direct effect *providing* that they comply with the *Van Gend* criteria.

(ii) Direct effect and regulations

Art 249 of the EC Treaty would appear to give regulations direct effect, providing as it does that a regulation '*shall be binding in its entirety and directly applicable in all Member States*'. It should be noted, however, that direct *applicability* can be distinguished from direct *effect*, despite the fact that the ECJ have used the terms interchangeably. (See Chapter 4, where it is explained that direct applicability should be interpreted as meaning that a provision requires no implementation or further action by the Member States in order to take effect.) While *all* regulations are directly applicable, the Court confirmed in Case 9/70, *Franz Grad*, that *regulations would be directly effective only when able to fulfil the Van Gend criteria.*

(iii)   Direct effect and decisions

Decisions, as regulations, are directly applicable, but Art 249 of the EC Treaty provides that they can be binding *only* upon those to whom they are addressed (whether that be Member States, corporations or individuals). The ECJ has held (see Case 9/70, *Franz Grad*) that decisions will be directly effective, providing they fulfil the *Van Gend* criteria, *but only against their addressees.*

(iv)   Direct effect of international agreements

This is a controversial and complex area, outside the scope of this book. It is sufficient to conclude that, in an attempt to ensure that Member States respect any commitments arising from agreements concluded with non-Member States, the ECJ has ruled that such agreements *may* have direct effect if circumstances are appropriate (see Case 104/81, *Kupferberg*).

(v)   Direct effect and directives

This has proved to be another rather controversial area. Article 249 of the EC Treaty provides that '*a directive shall be binding, as to the result to be achieved, upon each Member State to which it is addressed*'. Directives are therefore not directly applicable, as they require implementation before taking effect. Despite the wording of Art 249, which would appear to preclude directives from being directly effective, the ECJ have held that directives may indeed give rise to direct effects (see both *Franz Grad* and *Van Duyn*), arguing that this makes directives both more effective and also estops Member States from relying on their own 'wrongdoing' should they fail to incorporate a directive into domestic law.

This development of the doctrine has not been without its critics, who argue that to allow directives to be directly effective removes the distinction which it was intended should exist between regulations and directives.

The Court has confirmed that, in order for directives to be directly effective, they must be precise and unconditional but have also explained that *two additional criteria* must be fulfilled before directives can be directly effective, namely:

- The date for implementation must have passed.

  In Case 148/78, *Pubblico Ministero v Ratti (Ratti)*, the ECJ held that as directives provide Member States with a specific date by which they must be incorporated into domestic law, until that date has passed, Member States have complete discretion as to the choice, form and timing of the implementing legislation. *Once this date has passed, however, individuals will be able to rely on the provisions of a directive.*

- A directive will only be enforceable against the State.

  Before this criterion can be fully understood, it is necessary to understand the concepts of *vertical and horizontal direct effect*. Certain EC law provisions will place obligations on both the Member States *and* individuals. Providing the *Van Gend* criteria can be fulfilled, it may be possible for an individual to enforce such rights against another individual – a concept known as *horizontal direct effect*. Other EC law provisions (such as directives) only place obligations on the Member States. In such circumstances, it may be possible for an individual to enforce these rights against the State, again if the *Van Gend* criteria can be satisfied, but it will *not* be possible for any rights to be enforced against another individual. Such provisions will be said to be *vertically directly effective*.

In Case 152/84, *Marshall v Southampton and South West Hampshire AHA (Marshall No 1)*, the ECJ provided that, while directives place obligations on Member States, they place no obligations on individuals. It was therefore held that it is not possible to enforce a directive against an individual – that is, *horizontally* – although it is possible to enforce a directive against the State – that is, *vertically*.

In the above case, Miss Marshall wished to enforce rights emanating from the Equal Treatment Directive (Council Directive (76/297/EEC)) against her employer. She attempted to do this in the appropriate national court – an employment tribunal (ET). The ET made a preliminary reference to the ECJ (under Art 234 of the EC Treaty), asking whether she could rely on the Directive. The Court replied that she could do so, as she wished to rely on the provisions of the directive against the State who were one and the same as her employers. In other words, she could rely on the vertical direct effect of the Directive.

This requirement has the unfortunate effect of discriminating between individuals who wish to enforce their rights against the State as compared to those wishing to pursue their rights against an individual. The problem can be illustrated by consideration of Case 151/84, *Roberts v Tate & Lyle Industries* (the *Tate & Lyle* case), which mirrored the circumstances of *Marshall No 1*. Ms Roberts also wished to enforce rights emanating from the

Equal Treatment Directive but, as she was employed by a corporation as opposed to an organ of the State, her rights were unenforceable via the doctrine of direct effect.

What bodies are to be considered to be part of the State?

In an attempt to circumnavigate such problems, the ECJ have shown themselves willing to adopt the widest possible definition of 'State'. As already seen above, the ECJ has been willing to recognise an Area Health Authority as part of the State, while in Case 103/88, *Fratelli Constanzo*, regional and local government was also considered to be within the definition. In Case 222/84, *Johnston v Chief Constable of the RUC*, the Chief Constable was also recognised as being an 'emanation of the State'.

In Case C-188/89, *Foster v British Gas*, the ECJ provided that a 'Directive could be relied upon against organisations or bodies which were subject to the authority or control of the State or had special powers beyond those which result from the normal rules applicable to relations between individuals.' This judgment, while failing to provide an inclusive definition of 'State', has nevertheless proved helpful by making it clear that something more than mere control is necessary.

This conclusion is supported by the Court of Appeal's *dicta* in *Doughty v Rolls Royce* [1992] 1 CMLR 1045. Although Rolls Royce was, at the time, wholly owned by the Crown, it was not considered an emanation of the State, as the company neither provided a public service, nor had any of the 'special powers' referred to in *Foster*.

DEVELOPING THE EFFECTIVENESS OF COMMUNITY LAW

(i) Indirect effect

The ECJ's refusal to allow the horizontal direct effect of directives has without a doubt lessened their effectiveness. In an attempt at remedying this, the Court has developed a principle which has become known as *indirect* effect or '*the interpretive obligation*'.

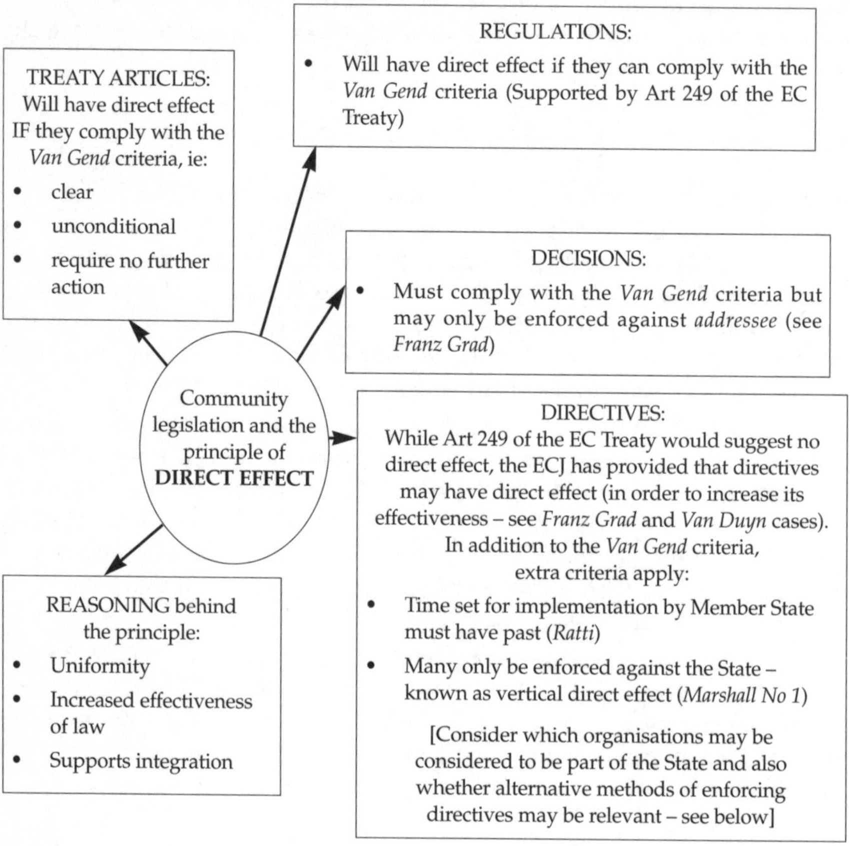
REGULATIONS:
• Will have direct effect if they can comply with the *Van Gend* criteria (Supported by Art 249 of the EC Treaty)
TREATY ARTICLES:
Will have direct effect IF they comply with the *Van Gend* criteria, ie:
• clear
• unconditional
• require no further action
DECISIONS:
• Must comply with the *Van Gend* criteria but may only be enforced against *addressee* (see *Franz Grad*)
Community legislation and the principle of **DIRECT EFFECT**
DIRECTIVES:
While Art 249 of the EC Treaty would suggest no direct effect, the ECJ has provided that directives may have direct effect (in order to increase its effectiveness – see *Franz Grad* and *Van Duyn* cases).
In addition to the *Van Gend* criteria, extra criteria apply:
• Time set for implementation by Member State must have past (*Ratti*)
• Many only be enforced against the State – known as vertical direct effect (*Marshall No 1*)
[Consider which organisations may be considered to be part of the State and also whether alternative methods of enforcing directives may be relevant – see below]
REASONING behind the principle:
• Uniformity
• Increased effectiveness of law
• Supports integration

The Direct Effect of Community Legislation

The basic principle

In Case 14/83, *Von Colson*, the ECJ reminded Member States of their duty under Art 10 of the EC Treaty (then Art 5), namely '*to ensure the fulfilment of the obligations ... resulting from action taken by the institutions of the Community*'. The Court went on to explain that such obligations also bind all the authorities of Member States '*including, for matters within their jurisdiction, the courts*'. Consequently, an obligation is placed on national courts to *interpret and apply* national law in a manner which is consistent with the wording and purpose of directives.

This judgment has been the subject of much academic criticism as it requires national courts to supplement the role of the domestic legislator. The principle has also been criticised for allowing the direct effect of directives via the 'back door', without the need to ensure that the restrictive *Van Gend* criteria can be fulfilled.

The principle has, however, undoubtedly succeeded in enhancing the effectiveness of *unimplemented and incorrectly implemented directives* while at the same time placing another obstacle in the path of Member States who may fail to comply with their obligations.

The development of the doctrine of indirect effect

The *Von Colson* judgment left a number of questions unanswered with regard to the *exact extent* of the principle of 'indirect effect'. Subsequent

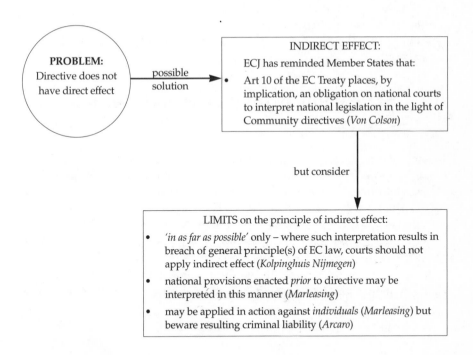

The Doctrine of Indirect Effect of Directives

decisions have made it clear that there are *limits* on the application of the principle.

In Case 80/86, *Kolpinghuis Nijmegen*, the Court made it clear that it would not be possible to interpret national legislation in the light of a directive should this result in conflict with any of the general principles of Community law, such as non-retroactivity or legitimate expectation (see Chapter 4 for consideration of the general principles). Thus, national courts must only interpret national law to conform with Community directives, but *only 'in so far as it is possible'* and the ECJ has, in general, shown itself content to rely on the discretion of national courts in this matter.

In Case C-106/89, *Marleasing*, the ECJ confirmed that national legislation, which has been interpreted by a national court in the light of a non- or incorrectly implemented directive, can be relied on not only by an individual against the State, but also against another individual and *even where such national law had been enacted prior to the directive and was not intended to implement it*. (However, it appears that this decision was tempered in Case C-168/95, *Luciano Arcaro*, where the ECJ provided that national courts were not obliged to follow *Marleasing* if criminal liability could result.)

(ii) State liability for damages (*Francovich* damages)

In view of the limitations placed on the direct effect of directives and despite the possibility of enforcing rights under the principle of indirect effect, a number of barriers may *still* exist with regard to the enforcement of rights emanating from a directive. (There may be no national law to interpret or interpretation may simply not be possible.)

In Cases C-6/90 and C-9/90, *Francovich and Bonifaci v Italy* (*Francovich*), the ECJ held that, should a Member State fail to incorporate a directive into national law, an individual who suffers damage as a consequence may claim compensation from the State, thereby ensuring greater effectiveness of directives.

This right to compensation was, however, subject to a number of criteria, namely:

(i) the directive must confer a right on citizens;

(ii) the content of the right must be identifiable by reference to the directive;

(iii) there must be a causal link between the State's breach and the individual's damage.

The Court's judgment in *Francovich* reinforces the Member States' obligations under Art 10 of the EC Treaty and also provides a further incentive to Member States to ensure that EC law rights are not denied to citizens.

This ruling has been of immense importance to Community law and the principle has been clarified and extended in a number of later cases particularly Cases C-46/93 and C-48/93, *Brasserie du Pecheur SA v Germany* and *R v Secretary of State for Transport ex p Factortame Ltd and Others* (*Pecheur* and *Factortame*).

The development of State damages

In *Francovich*, the ECJ's decision related to a Member States failure to fulfil its obligations in relation to *directives* but, in *Pecheur* and *Factortame*, the ECJ took this a step further by providing that damages could also be available in situations where a Member State had breached rules contained within a *Treaty Article*. Once more, however, the Court explained that certain criteria must be fulfilled:

- the rule of law infringed must be intended to confer rights on individuals;
- the breach must be sufficiently serious;
- there must be a direct causal link between the breach and the damage caused.

The Court also provided that the principle applied to whichever organ of the State was responsible for the breach or omission, whether it be legislative, executive or judiciary.

The ECJ's interpretation of 'sufficiently serious'

With regard to what will constitute a 'sufficiently serious' breach, the Court has put forward various factors, which may be taken into account, including:

- the degree of clarity and precision of the EC rule that has been breached (if the rule is imprecisely worded, the breach will not be sufficiently serious, Case C-392/93, *R v HM Treasury ex p British Telecom*);
- the 'intentionality' or 'voluntariness' of the infringement and the damage caused (intentional fault is *not* essential, Case T-178, 179, 188–90/94, *Dillenkofer v Germany*);
- the degree of discretion provided to the Member State by the provision (where there is no, or limited, discretion, the infringement of law in itself

may be sufficient to establish the existence of a sufficiently serious breach, Case C-5/94, *R v MAFF ex p Hedley Lomas*).

It has also been made clear that the Court may inquire into whether the injured party had shown reasonable diligence to avoid the loss or damage or limit its extent and also whether that party had availed itself, in time, if all the other remedies open to it.

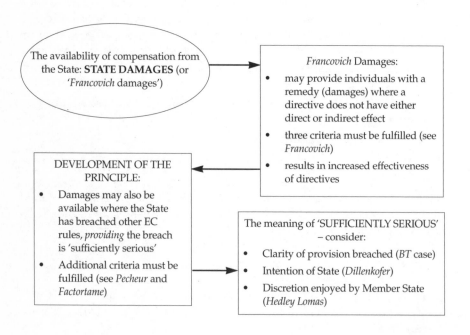

The availability of compensation from the State: **STATE DAMAGES** (or *'Francovich* damages')

Francovich Damages:

- may provide individuals with a remedy (damages) where a directive does not have either direct or indirect effect
- three criteria must be fulfilled (see *Francovich*)
- results in increased effectiveness of directives

DEVELOPMENT OF THE PRINCIPLE:

- Damages may also be available where the State has breached other EC rules, *providing* the breach is 'sufficiently serious'
- Additional criteria must be fulfilled (see *Pecheur* and *Factortame*)

The meaning of 'SUFFICIENTLY SERIOUS' – consider:

- Clarity of provision breached (*BT* case)
- Intention of State (*Dillenkofer*)
- Discretion enjoyed by Member State (*Hedley Lomas*)

The Remedy of STATE DAMAGES (or *Francovich* Damages)

(2) THE DOCTRINE OF SUPREMACY OF COMMUNITY LAW

Member States of the Community have two legal systems with which to contend – that of their own State and also that of the European Community. It therefore needs to be considered how the Member States are required to react should these sources of law conflict.

The creation of the doctrine

While the ECJ did not address the issue of supremacy of Community law directly in its *Van Gend en Loos* judgment, it did provide that Community law constitutes a *'new legal order ... for the benefit of which the States have limited their sovereign rights, albeit within limited fields'*.

It is clear from the Court's *dicta* that it was recognised that to allow Member States to apply conflicting national law, rather than Community would severely undermine the ability of the Community to achieve its aims. Thus, the doctrine of the supremacy (or primacy) of Community law was first (tentatively) established.

The development of the doctrine of supremacy

The precise implications of the doctrine of supremacy were not addressed until Case 6/64, *Costa v ENEL*. In its decision, the ECJ confirmed that where national law and EC law conflict, EC law must take precedence, even where the national law has been enacted subsequent to EC law – thus, ruling out the possibility of national law taking precedence under the concept of 'implied repeal'.

The Court provided a number of arguments in support of its *dicta*. First, it confirmed that EC law is an integral part of domestic legal systems, also providing that Member States had created this new legal system by limiting their sovereign rights and transferring power to the Community.

Drawing *heavily* on the spirit and aims of the Treaty, the Court pointed out that the *uniformity and effectiveness* of Community law would be jeopardised should national law be allowed to take precedence. In addition, the Court argued that the obligations undertaken by the Member States would be *'merely contingent'*, rather than *'unconditional'* could they *'be called into question by subsequent* (national) *legal acts'*.

The Court also referred directly to the text of the EC Treaty to support its judgment. Although the Treaty does not provide directly for the supremacy of Community law, the ECJ argued that Art 249 (then Art 189), which provides for the direct applicability of regulations, would be meaningless if Member States could negate their effect by enacting subsequent, inconsistent legislation.

While *Van Gend* and *Costa* dealt with the theoretical principle of supremacy, the Court had little to say on the practical application of the concept. A serious threat to the supremacy of EC law was revealed in Case 11/70, *Internationale Handelsgesellschaft*, when the German Administrative Court voiced its concern over the legal foundations on which the principle of supremacy was based. The German Court's disquiet revolved around their concern that fundamental rights contained within the German constitution could be overruled by Community law. The ECJ made it clear that EC law is supreme over all forms and sources of national law, softening the blow by declaring that the Community recognised such fundamental rights as an *'integral part of the general principles of law'*, whose protection would be ensured *'within the structure and objectives of the Community'*.

In Case 106/77, *Italian Minister of Finance v Simmenthal*, as a result of a preliminary reference the ECJ was required to consider whether a national court should disapply conflicting national legislation, even in situations where that court had no domestic jurisdiction to do so. (In Italy, this function was carried out by the Constitutional Court.) The ECJ provided that where conflict arises between national and Community law, the national court, under Community law, is required to give *immediate effect* to EC law and not wait for a ruling from the constitutional court.

This judgment is important, in that it confers on domestic courts jurisdiction that they may not have under domestic law. Once more, the ECJ emphasised the need for such action in order to ensure the *effectiveness* of Community law.

A further example of the jurisdiction of national courts being extended by Community law can be found in Case C-213–89, *R v Secretary of State for Transport ex p Factortame and Others (Factortame No 2)*. In this case, the ECJ explained that a national rule must be set aside by the national court if that rule prevents the court from granting interim relief. This can be seen as a further example of the practical consequences of the doctrine of supremacy.

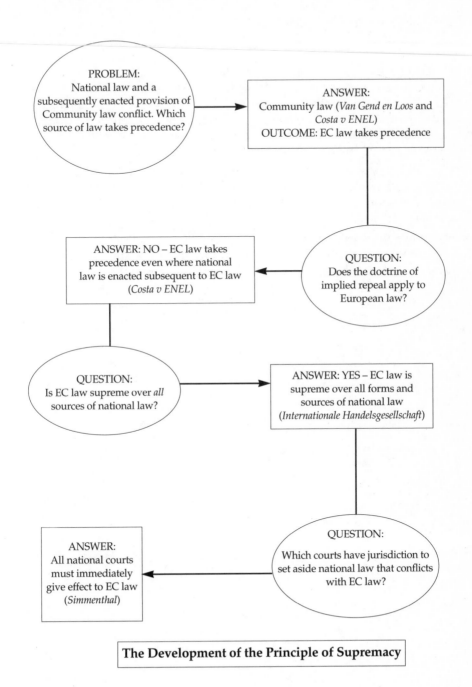

The Development of the Principle of Supremacy

CONCLUSIONS

Membership of the European Community has resulted in the Member States having an additional source of law to contend with – that of the EC. Rather surprisingly, the Treaties give little guidance as to the interaction between national and Community law and it has been left to the Court to interpreted which source of law is supreme in situations of conflict and also what effects EC law may have within the Member States.

The ECJ has reached the conclusion that EC law is not like other sources of international law. Not only is EC law supreme, but it also provides rights and obligations to Member States and individuals alike which can, in turn, be enforced before national courts.

While these principles may appear simplistic and obvious, their effect on the European Community has been profound: elevating its relevance and ensuring its uniform effectiveness throughout Europe.

6 Enforcing Community Law

In the preceding chapters, we have considered why the European Community (EC) was created and how it has developed. We have also considered who 'runs' the Community and the various sources of law that make up the Community's legal system. In Chapter 5, we also considered the relationship between national and Community law. In order to understand how the Community works in practice, we now need to consider how EC law is enforced.

Because Community law forms part of each Member State's domestic legal system, rights and obligations emanating from European law are normally *enforced before domestic courts,* rather than by the European Court of Justice (ECJ). We therefore need to consider exactly where and how such enforcement takes place.

The national courts are not, however, left totally to their own devices to deal with the application of EC law and so we will also consider the procedure known as 'preliminary reference' (Art 234 of the EC Treaty) which provides a valuable link between the ECJ and domestic courts.

While individuals will normally use domestic courts to enforce their EC law rights there are, however, certain actions that *only the ECJ (or CFI) has jurisdiction* to hear. These include 'infringement proceedings' against Member States who have failed to comply with their Community obligations (Arts 226–28 of the EC Treaty) and 'judicial review' of the acts and omissions of the Community institutions (Arts 230–33 of the EC Treaty). Each will be considered in turn.

(1) ENFORCING COMMUNITY LAW RIGHTS BEFORE NATIONAL COURTS

As we have already considered in Chapter 5, provided certain criteria are fulfilled, Community law has direct effect, that is it provides individuals with rights and obligations that are enforceable before national courts. We therefore need to consider which domestic courts may be employed, what procedures should be followed and what remedies should be available to individuals who wish to enforce their EC law rights.

Courts

It has been left to the Member States' discretion to designate which national courts will be appropriate to hear actions founded on Community law and also the procedures to be followed.

As the ECJ stated in Case 45/76, *Comet BV v Produktschap voor Siergewassen (Comet)*:

> It is for the domestic law of each Member State to designate the courts having jurisdiction and the procedural conditions governing actions at law intended to ensure the protection of the rights which subjects derive from the direct effects of Community law.

Procedures

The *dicta* in *Comet* demonstrates that the enforcement of *EC law* rights in national courts has to fit in with the national systems already in place for enforcement of *national* law.

Harmonisation of procedures throughout the EC is not practicable due to the wide variety of approaches enjoyed throughout the various Member States. Instead, in recognition of the Community's need to ensure the proper enforcement of EC law while still respecting the autonomy of the Member States, the ECJ has laid down a number of guidelines that the national courts are obliged to take into account. The first of these is the principle of non-discrimination.

In the *Comet* case, the Court's decision was contingent on 'it being understood that such conditions cannot be less favourable than those relating to similar actions of a domestic nature'.

This means that although the appropriate court and procedures are left up to the Member States, the States still have an obligation to ensure that national procedures do not discriminate against any individual wishing to enforce a EC law, rather than national law, right.

In addition, national procedures must not make it excessively difficult to obtain a remedy for a breach of EC law. In Case 199/82, *Amministrazione delle Finanze dello Stato v San Giorgio (San Giorgio)*, the ECJ explained that national rules and procedures must not make it, in practice, impossible for rights conferred by the Community to be exercised.

Remedies

The ECJ has been particularly careful to ensure that appropriate remedies are available with regard to breaches of Community law rules. In Case 33/76, *Rewe-Zentralfinanz v Landschwirtschaftskammer*, the Court explained that although it has been made possible for individuals to bring direct actions based on EC law before national courts, '*it was not intended to create new remedies in the national courts to ensure the observance of Community law*'.

This means that the remedies available for similar breaches of *national* law should be made available for breaches of *EC* law. However, once more, this has been qualified by guidelines laid down in decisions of the ECJ. The provision of a remedy must not discriminate and must be made available '*on the same conditions as would apply were it a question of observing national law*' (*Rewe-Zentralfinanz*). In addition, the remedy made available under national law must be *an effective remedy*.

In Case 14/83, *Von Colson*, the ECJ explained that Art 10 of the EC Treaty (then Art 5) provides Member States, and therefore their national courts, with the obligation of facilitating the achievement of the aims of the Community. Consequently, Member States and national courts must ensure that remedies available for breaches of EC law must be '*effective*', have a '*deterrent effect*' and be '*adequate in relation to the damage sustained*' (in other words, be proportionate).

The Court developed this principle in Case 222/84, *Johnston v Chief Constable of the RUC*, emphasising the need to ensure *effective judicial protection* for those who have suffered as a result of a breach of Community law. It was in Case C-271/91, *Marshall v Southampton and South West Hampshire AHA* (*Marshall No 2*), however, that the ECJ took the principle of effectiveness a step further.

In this case, they provided that not only did the remedy have to be comparable with that available for a similar breach of national law (*Comet* and *Rewe-Zentralfinanz*) but, if no *effective* remedy was available under national law, national courts should either improve upon what was available or devise a new, suitable remedy.

The development of a uniform Community remedy

In general, the Community has been happy to allow national courts to protect individuals Community law rights by means of appropriate national procedures and remedies. There has however been one exception to this: the development of the Community remedy of *State damages*.

The development of this remedy has been considered in some detail in Chapter 4. To briefly recap, in Cases C-6 and 9/90, *Francovich*, the ECJ provided that where a Member State had failed to correctly implement the aims of a directive, damages were available from the State to compensate those who had suffered loss as a result of the State's breach. This ensures that Member States may not rely on, or benefit from, their own wrong doings and that the remedy for doing so is uniform throughout the Community

The remedy is based on the obligations placed on Member States by Art 10 of the EC Treaty and has been developed in later cases (particularly Cases C-46 and 49/93, *Brasserie du Pecheur* and *Factortame No 3*) to include any sufficiently serious breach. A number of criteria must be fulfilled before damages can be made available and these too, are considered in Chapter 4.

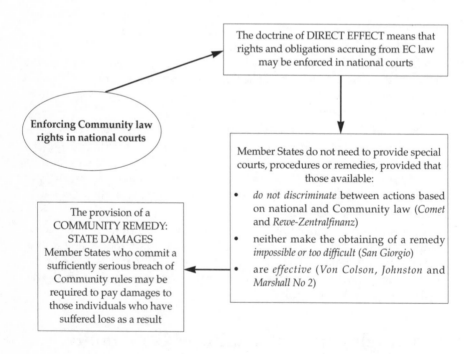

The doctrine of DIRECT EFFECT means that rights and obligations accruing from EC law may be enforced in national courts

Enforcing Community law rights in national courts

Member States do not need to provide special courts, procedures or remedies, provided that those available:

- *do not discriminate* between actions based on national and Community law (*Comet* and *Rewe-Zentralfinanz*)

- neither make the obtaining of a remedy *impossible or too difficult* (*San Giorgio*)

- are *effective* (*Von Colson*, *Johnston* and *Marshall No 2*)

The provision of a COMMUNITY REMEDY: STATE DAMAGES Member States who commit a sufficiently serious breach of Community rules may be required to pay damages to those individuals who have suffered loss as a result

Community Rights and National Courts

(2)   PRELIMINARY REFERENCES

Article 234 of the EC Treaty provides the ECJ with the jurisdiction to give preliminary rulings on the *interpretation* of the Treaty and also on the interpretation and *validity* of secondary legislation, when requested to do so by national courts.

The purpose of preliminary rulings

The purpose of Art 234 of the EC Treaty is to ensure the *uniform interpretation and application* of Community law by national courts. If interpretation were left to the domestic courts, it would not be possible to ensure uniformity, given that different legal systems employ different interpretive methods. (Consider, for example, the position in the UK, where the literal method of interpretation is favoured, as compared to other Member States, who employ the purposive method.)

The effects of preliminary rulings

The ECJ it is not bound by *precedent*. It does not have to follow its own previous rulings but in reality it does so in order to ensure consistency (for example, see the Court's *dicta* in Case 28–30/62, *Da Costa*, in which the ECJ repeated its *Van Gend* judgment).

A referring national court *will* however be bound by the ruling of the ECJ and is obliged to apply the ruling obtained to the case before them. While a ruling will normally be retrospective in its effect, the ECJ may limit the temporal effects of any such ruling (as it did in Case C-262/88, *Barber v Guardian Royal Exchange*, where the Court held that the ruling was effective only from the date of its judgment).

Despite national courts being bound by the ECJ, the Court has taken pains to point out that it is not in any way 'senior' to the national courts, but merely has a different function to the one that they perform. In reality however, the ECJ undoubtedly enjoys a superior position, employing national courts as enforcers and 'appliers' of Community law.

The consequences of the preliminary reference procedure

The availability of preliminary references has had a number of important consequences.

First, they have created a *link* between national legal systems and the EC legal system. Without such rulings, national courts and the ECJ would remain isolated from one another. Secondly, the availability of a reference affords national courts the opportunity to *familiarise* themselves with the Community legal order.

The impact of such rulings on the development of Community law should not be underestimated – consider such rulings as *Van Gend* and *Costa*, where the process has allowed the ECJ to develop a legal order and constitutionalise the Treaties by developing the doctrines of supremacy and direct effect.

In addition, preliminary references have been the vehicle by which the general principles of EC law have been articulated – see such decisions as *Kirk* – and, used in conjunction with Art 10 of the EC Treaty, the Court has also been able to extend the scope and effectiveness of the legal order. It is via Art 234 of the EC Treaty that the ECJ has been able to develop such principles as the 'interpretative obligation' (*Von Colson*) and 'State damages' (*Francovich*) and also to ensure that the remedies available for breach of Community law rights are effective (*Marshall No 2*).

Which national bodies may make a reference?

Article 234 of the EC Treaty provides that *'any court or tribunal of a Member State'* may make a reference. The ECJ has accepted references from a variety of courts and tribunals, including arbitration panels, insurance officers and administrative tribunals (the reference in *Van Gend* came from a Dutch Administrative Tribunal). Consideration of case law demonstrates, however, that the ECJ does not have the jurisdiction to accept a reference from a body that lies wholly or partially outside the legal systems of the Member States.

In Case 102/81, *Nordsee*, for example, a request for a ruling was made by an arbitration tribunal that had been established by contract – the reference was consequently refused. Conversely, in Case 246/80, *Broekmeulen*, the ECJ considered a Dutch body known as the Appeals Committee for General Medicine was an appropriate body, as it operated with the consent and co-operation of the public authorities and delivered decisions which were recognised as final.

The decision to refer

A national court or tribunal will only need to make a reference where it considers that its decision in the immediate case rests on a point of Community law. Article 234 of the EC Treaty makes it clear that it is for the national court to decide when a reference is to be made and *not* the parties to a case or any other party or authority, including the ECJ. (National precedent should never operate to prevent a court from seeking a ruling, see Cases 166 and 146/73, *Rheinmuhlen-Dusseldorf*.) The Treaty also distinguishes between those national courts that have the *discretion* to refer and those that are *obliged* to.

(i)   The discretion to refer

Article 234(2) provides that any court 'may, if it considers that a decision on the question is necessary to enable it to give judgment, request the Court of Justice to give a ruling thereon.' The ECJ has interpreted this to mean that where an appropriate body is called upon to reach a decision which is based on an issue of Community law, that body has the right to make a reference to the ECJ (*Simmenthal*). It should be noted however, that where the action concerns the validity of secondary legislation such discretion will be lost unless the court is satisfied that the Community act is valid. This is because the ECJ alone has the jurisdiction to declare a Community act invalid (Case 314/85, *Foto-Frost*).

(ii)   The obligation to refer

Article 234(3) of the EC Treaty provides that national courts or tribunals *'against whose decisions there is no judicial remedy in national law ... shall bring the matter before the Court of Justice'*. Thus, any court from which there is no appeal *must* make a reference when called upon to issue a judgment which depends upon a point of Community law. There are however, conflicting opinions as to which courts this applies.

Under what has become known as the 'abstract theory', it is provided that only courts from which there is *no* appeal will be obliged to refer. (In the UK, for example, Lord Denning in *Bulmer v Bollinger* (1974) 2 All ER 1226, CA, considered that only the House of Lords fell into this category.) Under the 'concrete theory', it is, however, thought that where the parties have *no automatic right* of appeal, the national court is obliged to refer. This theory is the most persuasive and supported by the ECJ, as can be evidenced by reference to *Costa v ENEL*.

It should be noted that there are three circumstances in which the ECJ have specifically held that it may *not be necessary* for a national court to make a reference. These circumstances were explained by the Court in Case 283/81, *CILFIT*, and are as follows:

- the question of EC law is irrelevant to the case being heard by the national court;

- the question of EC law has already been interpreted by the ECJ in a previous ruling (this principle was first established in *Da Costa*. As the ECJ does not have to follow its own previous rulings, national courts should, however, recognise the possibility that the ECJ may amend its original ruling and bear this in mind when taking their decision as to whether to refer or not);

- the correct interpretation is so obvious as to leave no scope for reasonable doubt (known as *acte clair* in the French legal system).

It should be noted that the ECJ has not precluded national courts from making a reference in the above circumstances, it has merely removed the obligation.

Can the ECJ refuse to provide a ruling?

As already considered, the decision to refer is the national courts' alone and may not be questioned by the ECJ. The ECJ has, however, on occasion, declined to give a ruling.

We have already considered instances where the Court has refused a ruling due to the fact that the national body making the ruling lay outside the Member State's legal system. In addition, in Cases 104/79 and 244/80, *Foglia v Novello (Nos 1 and 2)* the ECJ concluded that it has no jurisdiction to provide a ruling in a dispute which had been 'fabricated' by the parties, as their role was not to give abstract or advisory opinions. In Case C-83/91, *Meilicke*, the Court similarly concluded that it would exceed its jurisdiction if it answered hypothetical questions.

It has also withheld its opinion where proceedings have terminated in the national court (Case 338/85, *Pardini*) and also when it has felt that it has been given insufficient information or the question was too vague. (The Court has now issued guidance on this matter in *'Guidance on references by national courts for preliminary rulings'* ([1997] 1 CMLR 78).)

From examination of the above and other case law, it can be concluded that the ECJ may refuse to provide a ruling, but only in circumstances where to provide such a ruling would amount to an abuse of the preliminary reference procedure.

The referral procedure

Where a national court reaches the conclusion that a reference is necessary, it must formulate a question or questions to refer to the ECJ. Where such questions are in some way inappropriate, the Court, in the past, has shown itself willing to reformulate them in a manner that will best assist the national court, although there is growing evidence that the Court is becoming less willing to do so, due perhaps to pressure of work.

The national court will also need to provide issues of fact and national law relevant to the case in question. The national court will then stay proceedings until the ruling of the ECJ is transmitted back to it. It is important to remember that, while the ECJ has jurisdiction to pronounce on the validity of EC secondary legislation and interpret the Treaty, it is not the function of the Court to decide the outcome of the case before the national court. This function must be performed by the national court.

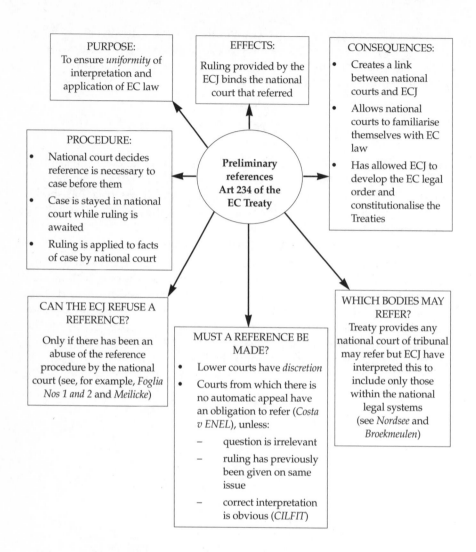

PURPOSE:
To ensure *uniformity* of interpretation and application of EC law

EFFECTS:
Ruling provided by the ECJ binds the national court that referred

CONSEQUENCES:
- Creates a link between national courts and ECJ
- Allows national courts to familiarise themselves with EC law
- Has allowed ECJ to develop the EC legal order and constitutionalise the Treaties

PROCEDURE:
- National court decides reference is necessary to case before them
- Case is stayed in national court while ruling is awaited
- Ruling is applied to facts of case by national court

Preliminary references
Art 234 of the EC Treaty

CAN THE ECJ REFUSE A REFERENCE?
Only if there has been an abuse of the reference procedure by the national court (see, for example, *Foglia Nos 1 and 2* and *Meilicke*)

MUST A REFERENCE BE MADE?
- Lower courts have *discretion*
- Courts from which there is no automatic appeal have an obligation to refer (*Costa v ENEL*), unless:
  - question is irrelevant
  - ruling has previously been given on same issue
  - correct interpretation is obvious (*CILFIT*)

WHICH BODIES MAY REFER?
Treaty provides any national court of tribunal may refer but ECJ have interpreted this to include only those within the national legal systems (see *Nordsee* and *Broekmeulen*)

(3) ENFORCEMENT ACTIONS AGAINST MEMBER STATES

Article 10 of the EC Treaty clearly provides all Member States with the duty to fulfil the specific obligations placed on them by both the Treaty and secondary sources of Community law. It also provides that the Member States may not to do anything that could jeopardise the aims of the Community. It is therefore necessary to consider how the Treaty ensures that all Member States comply with their Community obligations.

Actions brought by the Commission

Should a Member State breach its EC law obligations and an individual suffer as a result, that individual may, of course, bring an action against the errant State under the doctrine of direct effect (as discussed further in Chapter 5). The Treaty, however, provides its own methods of ensuring that Members States comply with their obligations.

The Treaty entrusts the Commission, under Art 211 of the EC Treaty, with the task of ensuring *'the proper functioning and development of the common market'*. This duty is expanded upon by Art 226 of the EC Treaty, giving the Commission the authority to investigate and, if necessary, bring before the ECJ any Member State that it considers has failed to fulfil its Treaty obligations. The Commission's powers are, however, discretionary and the Institution cannot be forced to act against a Member State (Case 48/65, *Lutticke*), although the Commission's conduct may be the subject of a complaint to the European Ombudsman (under Art 195 of the EC Treaty).

It is perfectly possible for an individual to bring an action against a Member State while, at the same time, the Commission is also initiating enforcement proceedings. This can be evidenced by the *Factortame* series of cases, together with Case C-246/89R, *Commission v UK*. Both acts and omissions of the Member States are open to scrutiny (Case 167/73, *Commission v France*).

Actions under Art 226 of the EC Treaty are initiated by the Commission, either on its own initiative or following a complaint. (It should be noted that the complainant does not play any further role in the proceedings as they are not intended as a means by which individuals can obtain redress.) Actions may be divided into two stages – the *administrative* stage and the *judicial* stage. The administrative stage can be further subdivided into the *informal* and the *formal*.

Where the Commission suspects a Member State is in breach of its Community obligations, the Commission will enter into (informal) dialogue with the appropriate authorities within that State. This stage is very important, as the majority of alleged breaches are resolved without the need for further intervention by the Commission. (It would appear that many States fail to comply with their obligations due to ignorance or misunderstanding and, in such circumstances, they are normally quick to remedy their breach.)

If the alleged breach is not rectified at this stage, the Commission may issue a *formal letter* defining the breach and requesting that the Member State submit its observations within a reasonable amount of time (normally two months). If the issue remains unresolved, as it will in only a minority of cases, the Commission will deliver a *'reasoned opinion'*, setting out how the Member State has violated Community law and allowing Member States a reasonable time (again usually two months, but this will depend on individual circumstances) to remedy the alleged breach.

The reasoned opinion is very important in that it establishes the scope of the action and the legal arguments on which the Commission is relying. Should the Commission attempt to change its arguments at a later date, these will be rejected by the ECJ.

If the breach is not remedied within the stated time, the Commission will proceed to the *judicial* stage, referring the matter to the ECJ. Even at this stage, it may be possible to settle the action before the Court gives its judgment. Where judgment is given, only about one in 10 decisions favour the Member State. This is not surprising, as the Commission will not proceed if its case is weak. In addition, the ECJ has shown itself unreceptive to the majority of defences argued by the Member State.

In Case 128/78, *Commission v UK*, the *Tachograph* case, for example, the UK argued 'practical difficulties' due to trade union resistance to the introduction of tachographs in the cabs of lorries, while, in Cases 227–30/85, *Commission v Belgium*, it was argued that failure of regional, rather than central government had caused the breach. The Court accepted neither argument. In Case 101/84, *Commission v Italy*, Italy did not submit statistics required by the Community as a bomb attack on a data processing centre had destroyed relevant data. Italy argued *force majeure*, which was again not accepted by the Court. The ECJ did, however, concede that, in certain circumstances, this may provide an acceptable defence.

If the ECJ find that a Member State is in breach of its Community obligations, the Court will issue a declaration to that effect, requiring that the breach be remedied. Article 228 of the EC Treaty places an obligation on Member States to comply with the Court's judgment. Until amendments made to the EC Treaty by the Treaty on European Union (TEU) were introduced, a judgment of the ECJ was of declaratory effect only. The only remedy for failure to comply with such a judgment was for the Commission to initiate further enforcement procedures against reluctant Member States.

Under the amended Art 228, if rectification of the breach does not take place as soon as possible, the Commission is authorised to issue a further reasoned opinion, setting out the ways in which the Court's judgment has not been complied with (Art 228). This procedure may lead to the Commission once more bringing the errant Member State before the ECJ.

In such circumstances, the Commission is empowered to specify an appropriate pecuniary penalty that the Court may then impose on the State in an attempt to ensure that compliance is achieved as quickly as possible. This has had the effect of providing a rather toothless action with the necessary teeth, although it is not clear what the outcome would be if a

Member State refused to pay any fine imposed. This question has been the topic of academic debate, with a favourite suggestion being the removal of a defaulting Member State's voting rights within the Council.

Actions brought by Member States

If a Member State considers that another Member State has failed to fulfil its Community obligations, then the first State may bring the matter before the ECJ under Art 227 of the EC Treaty. Procedure first requires that the matter be brought to the attention of the Commission. The procedure followed will then mirror that of Art 226, other than the requirement that the Commission request the observations of both Member States.

The Commission is required to deliver its reasoned opinion within *three months* of the matter being brought to its attention. If the Commission fails to provide a reasoned opinion within this time, the complainant Member State may bring the matter before the ECJ. Should the Court find a violation, matters proceed as provided by Arts 226 and 228 of the EC Treaty, as discussed above.

Actions brought under Art 227 of the EC Treaty are extremely rare, with judgment only being reached on *one* occasion, in Case 141/78, *France v UK*. This is understandable, as Member States prefer to make an informal complaint to the Commission, rather than choose the far more politically contentious Art 227 procedure.

The effectiveness of enforcement procedures

As has already been touched upon above, the majority of actions are resolved at administrative stage (the Commission's 14th Annual Report (1996), for example, provides that, of 1,142 formal letters sent, only 93 resulted in referral to the ECJ). It can therefore be concluded that the procedure is successful from an 'educational' perspective, ensuring that Member States are aware of their obligations and comply without the need for judicial intervention.

Also important with regard to the effectiveness, or otherwise, of enforcement actions is the Commission's ability to uncover possible breaches, as the Commission has no 'police force' that it can enlist to assist. Often, a State's breach will be the result of their failure to implement directives and the Commission has sought to remedy this by requiring that directives be published in the Official Journal and also by insisting that Member States notify them when directives are incorporated into national law. The Commission has also employed technology by encourage citizens and companies to notify possible breaches on their website.

ARTICLE 226:
Provides Commission with the authority to investigate and bring before the ECJ any Member State it considers may be in breach of its obligations. It has two stages:

(I) ADMINISTRATIVE STAGE

- Informal – dialogue between Commission and State in an attempt to remedy breach

- Formal – letter sent to State, setting out breach and asking for observations within stated time

- Reasoned opinion – if breach still not remedied, Commission will issue reasoned opinion setting out what action State must take, by set date. If breach is not remedies by this date, Commission bring action before ECJ

(II) JUDICIAL STAGE

- If action is brought before ECJ, they will consider submissions of both parties

- Member State may put forward a defence but ECJ has generally shown itself unreceptive

ARTICLE 10:
Places Member States under a general obligation to take all appropriate measures to ensure fulfilment of Treaty aims

ENFORCEMENT ACTIONS against MEMBER STATES: Arts 226, 227 and 228 of the EC Treaty

ARTICLE 227:

- New Member State may bring another before ECJ

- State must first bring matter to the attention of the Commission who may take action over and issue 'reasoned opinion' within 3 months

EFFECTIVENESS of enforcement procedures:

- Administrative stage particularly successful – most breaches remedied here

- Art 227 unpopular

ARTICLE 228 – JUDGMENT AND BEYOND:

- If ECJ finds State has failed to fulfil its EC obligations, it will issue a judgment. State must comply as soon as possible

- Failure to comply may result in further action by Commission who may suggest pecuniary penalty be levied by Court

Enforcement Actions

It can be concluded that enforcement procedures, particularly the administrative stage of Art 226 of the EC Treaty, play an important role in ensuring that Community aims are achieved and Community law upheld.

Actions against the Community institutions

The Treaty provides the Community institutions with a number of powers and obligations. As in all developed legal systems, a mechanism has also been put into place through which the manner in which these obligations are discharged can be reviewed.

'Judicial review' is the term commonly used to describe a variety of causes of action relating to the review of acts or decisions of the Community institutions. It includes annulment actions (under Art 230 of the EC Treaty) and actions for failure to act (Art 232 of the EC Treaty). Judicial review also covers applications for interim measures relating to other judicial procedures (see Art 243 of the EC Treaty).

Actions to annul Community Acts (Art 230 of the EC Treaty)

Article 230 of the EC Treaty is the primary Community method by which the legality of the acts of the Community institutions may be challenged. If such a challenge is successful, the act will be declared void by the ECJ (Art 231 of the EC Treaty). This procedure is one of the 'checks and balances' which exist to ensure that Community institutions act within the limits of the powers afforded them by the Treaties.

Whose acts may be challenged?

Article 230 of the EC Treaty refers to 'acts adopted jointly by the European Parliament and the Council, acts of the Council, of the Commission and of the ECB ... and of the European Parliament intended to produce legal effects vis à vis third parties. Prior to amendments introduced by the TEU, the Treaty only referred to acts adopted by the Council and the Commission. The ECJ had, however, already declared the acts of the European Parliament (EP) to be reviewable prior to such amendments (see Case 294/83, *Parti Ecologiste 'Les Verts' v EP* – both this decision and the subsequent Treaty amendments can be seen as an example of the increasing recognition of the importance of the role played by the EP within the Community).

Which acts may be challenged?

Consideration of the wording of Art 230 of the EC Treaty reveals that acts (regulations, decision and directives) other than recommendations and opinions may be challenged. The ECJ have interpreted this to include *any act which is capable of having legal effects* (see, for example, Case 22/70, *Commission v Council*, the *ERTA* case).

Grounds for bringing a challenge

The Treaty specifies the following grounds under which an action may be brought:

- *lack of competence* – this occurs where the community institutions act in areas where they are not authorised to do so by the Treaty;

- *infringement of an essential procedural requirement* – for example, the Council failing to consult the EP, as in Case 138/79, *Roquette Freres v Council*;

- *infringement of the Treaty or any rule of law relating to its application* – this ground often overlaps with others. The ECJ has explained that it can include a breach of one of the General principles of Community law, see Case 4/73, *Nold v Commission*;

- *misuse of powers* – this ground will be relevant where an institution has used its power(s) for an improper purpose.

Who can bring such an action?

This has proved to be a controversial area and often the subject of examination questions. Applicants can be divided into those with automatic *locus standi* and those who have to prove sufficient interest and can be categorised as follows.

Privileged applicants

The Treaty gives automatic *locus standi* to Member States, the Council and Commission.

Semi-privileged applicants

In cases where their prerogatives (rights or interests) are clearly affected, the Treaty provides that the EP, Court of Auditors (CoA) and European Central Bank (ECB) may commence an action. As already discussed above, the position of the EP as a litigant was amended by the TEU. While the ECJ had already accepted Parliament's right to bring an action in Case C-70/88, *European Parliament v Council* (the *Chernobyl* case), it was not until the TEU came into force that this was formalised. The extent of the EP's prerogatives is not entirely clear, but the ECJ has demonstrated that it is prepared to interpret Art 230(3) of the EC Treaty widely.

Non-privileged applicants

The Treaty provides that any natural or legal person may bring an action where he is the addressee of a decision and there is little problem demonstrating *locus standi* in such a situation.

However, the Treaty also provides that where a decision has been addressed to another person OR the act in question is a regulation, which in the circumstances is equivalent to a decision, that person may bring an action *providing* that it can be demonstrated that the act affects him both directly and individually.

It, therefore, needs to be considered how 'direct and individual concern' has been interpreted by the Court in relation to both decisions and regulations.

(i)   Individual concern

Where the act in question is a decision addressed to another, the ECJ developed a 'test' in Case 25/62, *Plaumann v Commission*.

In that case, the applicant was an importer of clementines. He sought to challenge a decision addressed to the German Government, as it allowed them to reduce the duty on clementines imported from outside the EC. The ECJ prescribed that, in order to demonstrate 'individual concern', the applicant must be able to demonstrate that he is *distinguishable from other persons generally*, due to certain attributes or circumstances – in this case, he had to show he was a member of a 'closed class'. In addition, he should be able to demonstrate that, by virtue of these attributes or circumstances, he should be singled out in the same way as the addressee.

He failed in his action because, as the Court pointed out, any other person could carry out the commercial activity in which he was involved. This test has been criticised as unduly restrictive, but *Plaumann* remains the seminal case in this area.

Where the legislative act is a regulation, the Court has, on occasion, applied the same 'closed category' test as in *Plaumann*. This approach was taken in Cases 789 and 790/79, *Calpak*, where the ECJ also explained that the Court intended to look behind the *form* of the act to the *substance* to determine its true nature.

(ii)   'Direct' concern

Where an applicant succeeds in demonstrating 'individual concern', he must then prove that the act was of 'direct concern'.

The Court have provided that there must be a direct causal link between the act and the impact on the applicant – see, for example, Cases 41–44/70, *International Fruit Co v Commission*.

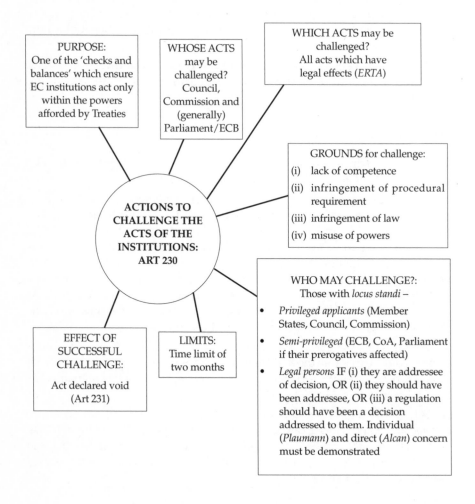

Judicial Review of the Acts of EC Institutions

Other limits on actions

The Treaty imposes a time limit of two months on the bringing of an action. This time starts to run either from the publication of the measure, of its notification to claimant, or of the day on which it came to the knowledge of claimant.

Effects of annulment

Article 231 of the EC Treaty provides that if the Court finds an application for annulment well founded, the act should be declared *void*. Normally, nullity will be considered to be retroactive although the Court has shown itself willing to limit the temporal effects in appropriate circumstances, particularly where an innocent party may otherwise suffer loss (see, for example, Case 81/72, *Commission v Council*).

Under Art 233 of the EC Treaty, institution(s) are obliged to act to comply with the judgment of ECJ. The Treaty does not provide any sanction should an institution fail to comply with a judgment (unlike the position where a Member State fails to comply), although by failing to comply, an institution may find itself vulnerable to *claims for damages* under Art 288 of the EC Treaty, which is discussed in further detail below.

Judicial Review of the Acts of EC Institutions

Actions against institutions for failure to act (Art 232 of the EC Treaty)

Actions under Art 232 of the EC Treaty can be seen as the other side of the coin from Art 230 of the EC Treaty actions. While the latter renders acts of the institutions ineffective, the former may be used to compel an institution to fulfil its Community obligations. An action will only be available where the applicant can show that such an obligation exists.

Whose failure to act can be challenged?

Article 232 of the EC Treaty clearly provides that '*Should the European Parliament, the Council or the Commission, in infringement of this Treaty, fail to act*', an action may be brought before the ECJ. Action may also be brought against the ECB, as prescribed by Art 232(4) of the EC Treaty.

Who may make a challenge?

The Treaty provides the Member States and all institutions with automatic *locus standi*. The ECB may also bring an action if it can be shown that it relates to an area falling within the Bank's *'field of competence'*. Natural and legal persons once more have limited *locus standi* and may only bring an action where an institution had an obligation to address an act (other than an opinion or a recommendation) to him or her. The applicant must demonstrate direct and individual concern and the Court will apply the same restrictive tests as have been established for Art 230 of the EC Treaty (Case C-107/91, *ENU v Commission*).

Procedure in Art 232 of the EC Treaty

Actions will only be admissible where the institution has first been *called upon to act* by the challenger, thus providing the institution concerned with the opportunity to remedy its alleged omission.

Once a request for action has been made, the institution must then define its position within *two months* of being called upon to act. Once an institution has defined its position, no further action is possible (Case 48/65, *Alfons Lutticke v Commission*) although the ECJ has, on occasion, been willing to accept a challenge to the definition itself, under Art 230 of the EC Treaty (see, for example, Case 191/82, *Seed Crushers and Oil Producers Association v Commission*).

If the institution does not define its position, any action is then subject to a time limit of a further two months.

Consequences of a successful action

Article 233 of the EC Treaty provides that institutions are obliged to comply with the Court's ruling under Art 232 of the EC Treaty.

Other actions against the institutions

It should now be obvious that bringing an action under either Art 230 or 232 of the EC Treaty can present particular problems for individuals, both natural and legal, due to the difficulties associated with proving *locus standi*. It is therefore important to consider how individuals may be able to achieve the same effect as available through Arts 230 and 232, but via other means.

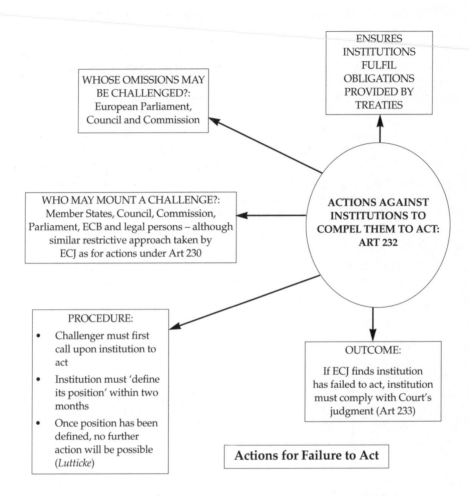

Actions for Failure to Act

We have already considered the *preliminary reference* procedure (Art 234 of the EC Treaty), which allows national courts to question the validity of Community acts. While preliminary references do not provide individuals with a direct action they may, never the less, provide a channel through which a challenge may be mounted and as such are worth bearing in mind.

In addition, there are a number of other actions through which an individual may challenge a Community act and each is briefly considered below.

Plea of illegality (Art 241 of the EC Treaty)

Article 241 of the EC Treaty provides a means of *indirect* challenge against a Community *regulation*, but once more, the Court will look at the substance rather than the form of the act (Case 92/78, *Simmenthal*). The fact that the act has been labelled something other than a regulation will not, therefore, be decisive.

A plea of illegality is *not* an independent action (Cases 31 and 33/62, *Wohrmann and Lutticke v Commission*). It is only available incidentally, where other proceedings have been brought before the ECJ, and the ECJ has explained that the purpose of the action is to allow an individual protection from the application of an illegal regulation. The action may be pleaded on the same *grounds* as those found under Art 230 of the EC Treaty.

The *effect* of a successful challenge is that the regulation will be declared *inapplicable* in that case, but it will not be declared void. Any measures based on the regulation will however be automatically void and subsequent measures based on the regulation will also be subject to challenge.

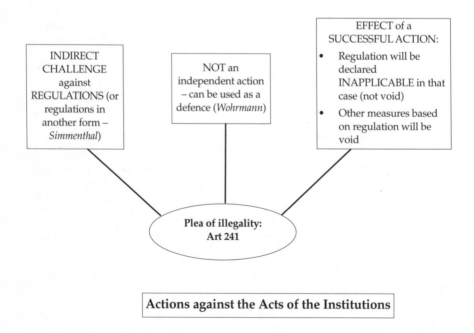

INDIRECT CHALLENGE against REGULATIONS (or regulations in another form – *Simmenthal*)

NOT an independent action – can be used as a defence (*Wohrmann*)

EFFECT of a SUCCESSFUL ACTION:
- Regulation will be declared INAPPLICABLE in that case (not void)
- Other measures based on regulation will be void

Plea of illegality: Art 241

Actions against the Acts of the Institutions

Actions for damages (Art 288 of the EC Treaty)

Article 288(1) of the EC Treaty provides that the *'contractual liability of the Community shall be governed by the law applicable to the contract in question'*. When an individual wishes to make a claim against a Community institution for damages in relation to a contractual matter, the action must, therefore, be brought in the appropriate national court and under the legal rules appropriate to that Member State.

Article 288(2) of the EC Treaty relates to the Community's *non-contractual* liability. Under the jurisdiction afforded it by Art 235 of the EC Treaty, the ECJ may hear actions brought against the Community in relation to damage caused by its institutions and the ECB (*fautes de service*) or by its servants (*fautes personnelles*) in the performance of their duties. (Note that jurisdiction has since been transferred to the Court of First Instance.)

Actions brought under Art 288 are independent actions and there is no limitation on *who* may bring such an action (*Lutticke*). There is, however, a *time limit* of five years from time of injury, or from the time which the claimant should have reasonably known of it, has been imposed. *Fault*, *damage* and *causation* must be proven and as such, an Art 288 action is essentially similar to the English concept of tort.

With regard to liability in relation to *'servants in the performance of their duties'*, the Community and its institutions may be deemed liable under the concept of *vicarious liability*. The concept of vicarious liability has been interpreted far more restrictively under Community law than is usual under English law and the range of acts performed by staff for which the Community will accept liability is narrow. (This can be evidenced by consideration of Case 9/96, *Sayag v Leduc*.)

Injurious acts may either be of an administrative or legislative nature and each needs to be considered in turn with regard to the proving of 'fault'.

(i) Administrative acts

Where an action is brought in relation to *the manner in which Community rules have been applied* or the manner in which staff have carried out their duties, the Community, via the appropriate institution(s) and staff, may be liable for both wrongful acts and omissions.

'Fault' (or 'illegality' as it is sometimes termed) may involve negligence, the failure to consider relevant facts, to accord individuals certain procedural rights or to adequately supervise bodies to whom power has been delegated, etc. The relative seriousness of the 'error' may be taken into account and, for an example of the Court's thinking in this area, see Case 145/83, *Adams v Commission*.

(ii) Legislative acts

Where the act complained of is legislative in nature (once again the substance of the act, rather than the form will be definitive), the Court has developed a 'formula', laying down the general conditions which must exist before liability can be found. This formula has become known as the '*Schoppenstedt* formula' following Case 5/71, *Schoppenstedt v Commission* and involves the following considerations:

- does the legislative act involve choices (discretion) of economic policy, on the part of the Community authorities? If *yes*;
- has there been a breach of a superior rule of law intended for the protection of individuals? If yes;
- is the breach 'sufficiently serious'?

A 'superior rule of law' may be a general principle of Community law, such as non-discrimination or legal certainty. Whether the breach was 'sufficiently serious' (or 'manifest and grave') will depend on a number of factors being taken into consideration. These are likely to include the clarity of the rule that was breached, the amount of discretion enjoyed by the authorities, whether the error was excusable and whether the breach was voluntary or intentional (see Cases C-46 and 48/93, *Brasserie du Pecheur v Germany* and *R v Secretary of State for Transport ex p Factortame*).

In addition to proving fault, a claimant must also demonstrate causation and damage. With regard to causation, the Court has made it clear that the applicant must demonstrate two things:

- Community action caused the loss/damage;
- the chain of causation has not been broken.

With regard to the second element, the chain of causation may be broken by the actions of a Member State, in which case, it will be the State, as opposed to the Community, that will be liable – unless the Community has failed to adequately exercise its supervisory power over the State (*Lutticke*). (If there is joint liability on the part of the Community and a Member State, the Member State will generally be considered primarily liable and the action should then be brought in the appropriate national court.) Contributory negligence may also serve to defeat a claim or at least reduce the quantum of damages (*Adams*).

Article 288 of the EC Treaty provides that the Community must make good *'any damage'* caused by its institutions or staff. This has been read restrictively by the Court who have held that the amount claimed must be actual, certain and concrete (Case 26/74, *Roquette Freres v Commission*) and compensation is therefore unlikely to be awarded for losses such as anticipated profits.

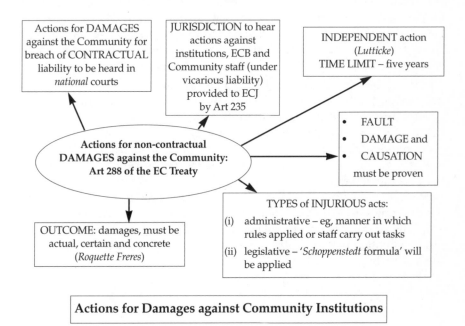

Actions for DAMAGES against the Community for breach of CONTRACTUAL liability to be heard in *national* courts

JURISDICTION to hear actions against institutions, ECB and Community staff (under vicarious liability) provided to ECJ by Art 235

INDEPENDENT action (*Lutticke*) TIME LIMIT – five years

Actions for non-contractual DAMAGES against the Community: Art 288 of the EC Treaty

- FAULT
- DAMAGE and
- CAUSATION

must be proven

OUTCOME: damages, must be actual, certain and concrete (*Roquette Freres*)

TYPES of INJURIOUS acts:

(i) administrative – eg, manner in which rules applied or staff carry out tasks

(ii) legislative – '*Schoppenstedt* formula' will be applied

Actions for Damages against Community Institutions

CONCLUSIONS

Community law places rights and obligations on individuals, Member States and Community institutions alike. European law would, however, have little effect if such rights and obligations were unenforceable, and so the Community legal system includes a variety of means by which it can be ensured that all comply with EC law.

When an individual (natural or artificial) breaches Community law, he can expect to have an action brought against him in an appropriate national court under the doctrine of direct effect, with domestic courts being 'assisted' by the ECJ under the preliminary reference procedure. It should be remembered that the ECJ's role does not allow it to take over the proceedings and their role is restricted to providing an interpretation of Community law and/or judgment as to the validity of legislative acts of the institutions.

When a Member State breaches its obligations, the Treaty provides that the Commission or a second Member State may bring an action before the ECJ in order to ensure compliance. In addition, a Member State may find itself a defendant in an action before a national court under the doctrine of vertical direct effect and/or, where the claimant wishes to pursue and action for damages, under the principle of 'State damages' (*Francovich* damages). Often, Member States will find themselves the subject of an action brought by an individual in a national court, while *at the same time* being the subject of an enforcement action by the Commission/Member State.

Other than in actions relating to contractual liability, Community institutions will be brought before the ECJ/CFI should they breach Community rules. Any challenge to the validity of legally effective acts of the institutions will normally be brought under Art 230 of the EC Treaty (judicial review), although due to the difficulties associated with proving *locus standi*, individuals should also consider the possibility of employing the preliminary reference, plea of illegality and/or 'action for damages' procedures to mount a challenge. Special notice should however be taken of the differing effects of these actions, with actions under Art 288 of the EC Treaty being the only action that provides a right to compensation. It should not be forgotten that institutions may be compelled to act under Art 232 of the EC Treaty.

Challenging INSTITUTIONS in relation to *secondary legislation* and other acts having legal effects by:

- Member States, other institutions and individuals via judicial review (Arts 230 and 232 in ECJ)
- Individuals via preliminary reference (Art 234, at discretion of national court, ECJ involvement re preliminary reference)
- Individuals via plea of illegality (Art 241 – indirect in ECJ)
- Individuals via claim for non-contractual damages (Art 288)

Challenging MEMBER STATES for not fulfilling their EC obligations by:

- Individuals via vertical direct effect, indirect effect, State damages (in national court, preliminary reference may result)
- Commission via enforcement action (Art 226 in ECJ)
- Other Member State via enforcement action (Art 227 in ECJ)

Possible alternatives:

- Complaint to Euro Parliament/Euro Ombudsman
- CoA may investigate financial irregularities
- Euro Parliament may challenge Commission

Challenging INDIVIDUALS for breaching EC law by:

- Other individuals via horizontal direct effect, indirect effect (in national court but preliminary reference may result)
- Commission re EC competition law (Arts 81 and 82)

ENFORCING EUROPEAN LAW

7 Free Movement of Goods

As previously discussed, the European Communities were created in an attempt to ensure peace and economic stability within Europe and the EC Treaty sets out a number of aims to be achieved in order that these aspirations be fulfilled.

While the majority of these aims may be categorised as economic, others have social impacts, while others still can be said to be political in nature. Economic integration is, however, traditionally seen as the primary goal of the Community and the objective of creating a *common market* has been explicitly set out under Art 2 of the EC Treaty. Article 3 of the EC Treaty enlarges upon this by providing a list of activities that the Community must put into effect in order to ensure that Community aims are achieved. Article 3(c) of the EC Treaty, in particular, provides that the Community must ensure that all *'obstacles to the free movement of goods, persons, services and capital'* are abolished. These have commonly become known as the 'four freedoms' and it is the first of these freedoms with which this chapter is primarily concerned.

Creating an area that has 'free movement of goods' cannot be achieved overnight and the rules concerning its creation and maintenance are often complex. Such rules can be best understood if an incremental approach is taken and, in this chapter, we will consider some of the more important rules which apply to *Member States* with regard to the removal of both pecuniary and non pecuniary barriers to trade.

(1) PECUNIARY BARRIERS TO TRADE

It should be remembered that prior to the Community's inception each Member State levied, on importers and exporters, customs duties on goods entering and leaving each State. In order to create an area where trade was facilitated rather than hampered, customs duties had to be removed and a new system of regulation put into place.

(a) The creation of a customs union and common customs tariff (Arts 23 and 24 of the EC Treaty)

What the Treaty says

Article 23 of the EC Treaty provides that the Community is to be based on a *customs union*. The creation of a customs union involved the removal of all customs duties and all charges having equivalent effect, on goods moving between the Member States.

Article 23 of the EC Treaty also provides for the creation of a *common customs tariff* (CCT). The CCT is charged on all goods imported from outside the Community. It is charged at the same rate no matter which of the Member States the goods are imported into or where they are exported from.

Article 24 of the EC Treaty also provides that once non-domestic goods have been subject to the CCT, they shall be considered to be in free circulation and should be treated no differently than domestic goods. The CCT is a tariff raised by the EC, not Member States and, as such, forms part of the Community budget. It should not, consequently, be confused with charges levied by the Member States as part of their own internal taxation systems (which are discussed in further detail below).

The removal of existing customs duties was not, of course, achieved overnight and it was not until July 1968 that the final remaining customs duties were removed and the CCT introduced.

(b) The prohibition on new customs duties and charges having equivalent effect (Art 25 of the EC Treaty)

The removal of existing customs duties has the obvious benefit of allowing trade to take place on a level playing field, allowing the consumer to be the final arbiter as to which goods will be successful and which less so. The imposition of customs duties may however benefit Member States, allowing them an opportunity, for example, to promote domestically manufactured goods over foreign goods via the imposition of high import taxes. The possibility of a Member State imposing a new duty or charge could not, therefore, be ignored.

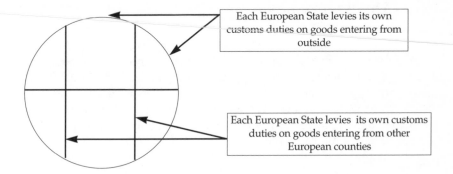

Each European State levies its own customs duties on goods entering from outside

Each European State levies its own customs duties on goods entering from other European counties

Europe PRIOR to the creation of the European Community

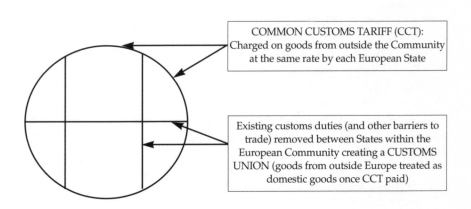

COMMON CUSTOMS TARIFF (CCT): Charged on goods from outside the Community at the same rate by each European State

Existing customs duties (and other barriers to trade) removed between States within the European Community creating a CUSTOMS UNION (goods from outside Europe treated as domestic goods once CCT paid)

The Common Customs Tariff and the Customs Union which now exist around and between the Member States

What the Treaty says

The removal of existing pecuniary barriers to trade would not, alone, have ensured the free movement of goods as it would not prevent Member States from *re-erecting* customs duties, or putting into effect other charges having equivalent effect, in circumstances considered beneficial to that State. Article 25 of the EC Treaty therefore provides that: *'Member States shall refrain from introducing between themselves any new customs duties on exports or any charges having equivalent effect.'*

The European Court of Justice's interpretation and application of Art 25 of the EC Treaty

Article 25 of the EC Treaty – *which applies to both imports and exports alike* – appears to provide reasonably clear instruction to Member States, but it has still been necessary for the European Court of Justice (ECJ) to interpret its exact meaning in order to ensure uniform application of its terms.

The term *'goods'* is not defined by the Treaty and it is has been necessary for the ECJ to consider exactly which goods may be subject to the EC's rules. It is obvious that the free movement of goods is fundamental to the achievement of Community aims and the ECJ has consequently provided a wide interpretation of the term. In Case 7/68, *Commission v Italy* (the *1st Art Treasures* case) the Court defined goods as including products which can be valued in money and which are capable of forming the subject of a commercial transaction.

The Court has also made it clear that the *purpose* for which the charge is levied is irrelevant and that it is the *effect* which is significant in deciding whether or not Art 25 applies (Case 24/68, *Commission v Italy*, the *2nd Art Treasures* case).

It has also been necessary for the Court to consider which charges will come within the scope of *'charges having equivalent effect'* (CHEEs). In the *2nd Art Treasures* case, the ECJ once again provided a wide definition, holding CHEEs to include *'any pecuniary charge ... imposed ... on domestic or foreign goods by reason of the fact that they cross a frontier'*.

The 'exceptions' to the rules

Once a tax or charge has been held to come within the scope of Art 25 of the EC Treaty, it is immediately deemed to be unlawful.

The Treaty does not provide for any derogation from the prohibition contained in Art 25, but the ECJ has explained that certain charges will *not* come within its scope. These include charges levied for a mandatory inspection and charges made for the provision of a commercial service.

Before such a charge will be considered to be outside the scope of Art 25 of the EC Treaty, a number of criteria that must firstly be fulfilled.

(i) Charges made for an inspection

Where a Member State levies a charge for an inspection, it will not constitute a CHEE provided it can satisfy the following conditions (Case 18/87, *Commission v Germany*, the *Animal Inspection Fees* case):

- the inspection is mandatory under *Community* law (see Case 46/76, *Bauhuis*);
- the inspection is non-discriminatory (that is, both domestic and imported goods treated alike);
- the inspection is in the interest of the Community and promotes the free movement of goods;
- the charge does not exceed the cost of the inspection;
- the charge is proportionate to quantity of the goods inspected and not their value (see Case 87/75, *Bresciani*).

(ii) Charges levied for a service provided

Where a Member State has levied a charge for a service performed, that charge will not be considered to be a CHEE if the following criteria can be fulfilled:

- the service rendered a *specific benefit* to the importer/exporter (Case 24/68, *Commission v Italy*, the *Statistical Levy* case);
- the charge is proportionate to quantity, not value, of the goods to which the service has been rendered (see Case 87/75, *Bresciani*);
- the charge does not exceed the cost of the inspection (*Bresciani*);
- both domestic and imported goods are treated alike (*Bresciani*).

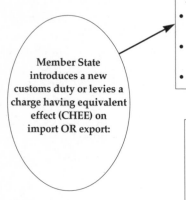

ARTICLE 25 of the EC Treaty:

- *Prohibits* all new customs duties and charges having an equivalent effect
- Any duty/charge will be illegal and will normally have to be refunded (*San Giorgio*)
- Art 25 has direct effect (*Van Gend*)

Member State introduces a new customs duty or levies a charge having equivalent effect (CHEE) on import OR export:

BUT

ECJ has provided that the following will not be considered to be CHEEs and will not, therefore, be prohibited by Art 25:

- Charge for a mandatory inspection (*Animal Inspection* case)
- Fee for a service provided (if of specific benefit to importer/exporter) (*Statistical Levy* case)

PROVIDED that charge/fee is:

- Proportionate to the cost
- Based on quantity not quality
- Non-discriminatory (*Bresciani*)

The Prohibition on Pecuniary Barriers to Trade

(c)   The prohibition on discriminatory internal taxation (Arts 90 to 93 of the EC Treaty)

What the Treaty says

While Art 25 of the EC Treaty can be seen as preventing Member States levying duty by virtue of goods crossing a frontier, Art 90 of the EC Treaty provides that: *'No Member State shall impose, directly or indirectly, on the products of other Member States any internal taxation of any kind in excess of that imposed directly or indirectly on similar domestic products.'*

Both Articles are intended to ensure that trade between Member States is not distorted and Art 90 of the EC Treaty can be seen as complementing Art 25 of the EC Treaty by closing any loopholes which may exist. However, *internal taxation is only unlawful to the extent that it is discriminatory against imported products or protective of domestic products* and the Treaty does not seek to deprive Member States of the power to levy taxes for the purpose of raising public revenue.

The ECJ's interpretation of Art 90 of the EC Treaty

Clearly, there may be an argument as to what products may be considered to be 'similar'. In Case 27/67, *Fink-Frucht*, the ECJ provided that goods would be regarded as such if they came within the same tax classification but it has also been held that products need not necessarily be the same.

For example, in Case 170/78, *Commission v UK*, it was held that beer and wine are sufficiently similar to compete and it can be concluded that an appropriate test may be whether a consumer might substitute one product for the other for the purpose he has in mind. In Case 168/78, *Commission v France*, the *French Spirits* case, characteristics such as composition, physical characteristics and consumer usage were considered.

Indirectly discriminatory internal taxation

Taxation that is directly discriminatory overtly treats domestic and other goods differently but taxation that is *indirectly* discriminatory may, on the face of it, appear to comply with Community rules although in reality placing non-domestic goods at a disadvantage.

Case 112/84, *Humblot*, provides a good example of such treatment. French law decreed that the amount of car tax payable increased with the power rating of the vehicle, with cars below and above a 16CV rating being

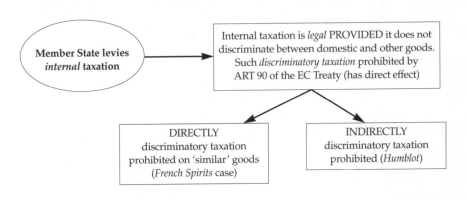

Internal Taxation Levied by the Member States

charged at different rates. No French car was rated above 16CV and therefore only imported cars fell into the higher tax rating. France's internal car taxation system was therefore considered to be covertly discriminatory.

Enforcing the rules relating to pecuniary barriers to trade

Article 25 of the EC Treaty has been held to be directly effective (*Van Gend*). Traders may therefore enforce their rights against a Member State, in the appropriate *national* court.

Member States will normally be required to repay any charges which have been unlawfully levied (Case 199/82, *Amministrazione delle Finanze dello Stato v San Giorgio*), unless that trader has passed the costs on to his customers (Cases C-192–218/95, *Société Comateb*).

In addition, an errant Member State may find itself the subject of an enforcement action brought by either the Commission or another Member State, before the ECJ (Arts 226–28 of the EC Treaty).

Article 90 of the EC Treaty is similarly directly effective (*Humblot*) and individuals may therefore enforce any rights accruing from the Treaty Article in their national courts. Once more, Member States who levy discriminatory internal taxation may also find themselves investigated by the Commission.

(2) THE ELIMINATION OF QUANTITATIVE RESTRICTIONS ON TRADE (ARTS 28–30 OF THE EC TREATY)

The problem

The prohibition of pecuniary barriers to trade would not, alone, be sufficient to guarantee the free movement of goods within the EC. In addition to the pecuniary measures discussed above, measures of a non-pecuniary nature can also hinder free movement.

Such non-pecuniary measures may include quantitative restrictions such as quotas, while the imposition of compulsory inspections or trading rules relating the composition, packaging, etc, of goods may also affect trade. The Treaty consequently provides a prohibition on quantitative restrictions and measures having equivalent effect, where such measures may affect trade.

What the Treaty says

Article 28 of the EC Treaty provides that: 'Quantitative restrictions on imports and all measures having equivalent effect shall be prohibited between Member States.' Article 29 of the EC Treaty provides a similar prohibition with regard to exports. Article 30 of the EC Treaty, on the other hand, provides derogation from both Arts 28 and 29. Such derogation – which may only be claimed in strictly limited circumstances – recognises, to a certain extent, the need for government regulation and the aim of free movement to be reconciled.

The attitude of the ECJ

As one would expect, each Member State has developed its own trading rules and, while the Community has attempted to harmonise such rules, progress has been slow. In the absence of harmonising legislation, the ECJ has taken the stance that such rules must not be allowed to hinder the free movement of goods, interpreting Arts 28 and 29 broadly to encompass as many restrictive measures as possible. On the other hand, Art 30 of the EC Treaty, which allows Member States to derogate, has been interpreted narrowly.

The following discussion relates largely to restrictions placed on *imports*. The position with regard to *exports* is discussed separately.

Quantitative restrictions

Quantitative restrictions can be described as national measures which impose a numerical limit on goods of a particular type, either entering or leaving a domestic market. The purpose of such behaviour is often to offer protection to domestic products. Both quotas and total bans fall within the scope of the term (see Case 2/73, *Geddo v Ente*, and Case 34/79, *R v Henn and Darby*).

Measures having equivalent effect

As well as prohibiting quantitative restrictions, Art 28 outlaws measures having equivalent effect (MHEEs). This term has proved difficult to define and has been the subject of both secondary legislation and numerous decisions of the ECJ. MHEEs can be seen, however, as including measures which may make importation more difficult or costly, or measures that promote or favour domestic goods.

(i) The Commission's view (secondary legislation)

Commission Directive (70/50/EEC) (OJ 1097 L13/29) was adopted in an attempt to amplify the meaning of Art 28 of the EC Treaty (then Art 30) and it is still used as a guide to the practices which are subject to Art 28.

With regard to MHEEs, the Directive makes an important distinction between two types of measures:

- *distinctly applicable measures* (DAMs) – measures which apply only to imports and are therefore discriminatory; and

- *indistinctly applicable measures* (IDAMs) – measures which are applicable to both domestic and imported products alike and which, therefore, do not appear to be discriminatory.

The Commission, via the Directive, concluded that while DAMs would come within the scope of Art 28, IDAMs would not normally do so.

(ii) The jurisprudence of the ECJ

Whose 'measures' will be caught?

The Court has provided a wide interpretation with regard to *whose* measures may be caught by Art 28 of the EC Treaty, which is primarily addressed to Member States.

In Case 113/80, *Commission v Ireland*, the *Buy Irish* case, the ECJ held that the Irish Government's support of the Irish Goods Council's campaign was sufficient to allow the body to be considered 'public' for the purposes of Art 28 of the EC Treaty.

In Case C-265/95, *Commission v France*, the Court went even further by declaring that the actions of French farmers, who had disrupted imports, came within the ambit of the French Government, as the State authorities were considered not to have taken sufficient action to ensure free movement.

Judicial development of Art 28

The Court's jurisprudence has been responsible for the development of Art 28 of the EC Treaty into a formidable tool in the drive against national rules which restrict the free movement of goods. In an attempt to illustrate this development, the Court's decisions will be considered in chronological order.

'The *Dassonville* formula'

While Directive 70/50/EEC provided that IDAMs (non-discriminatory measures) do not normally come within the scope of Art 28 of the EC Treaty, the ECJ have held, in Case 8/74, *Procureur du Roi v Dassonville*, that: '*All trading rules enacted by Member States which are capable of hindering directly or indirectly, actually or potentially, intra-Community trade are to be considered as measures having an effect equivalent to quantitative restrictions.*'

In what has become the *authoritative definition of an MHEE*, the Court interpreted Art 28 of the EC Treaty to bring IDAMs as well as DAMs within its scope. In *Dassonville*, the ECJ also provided that it is not necessary to show an actual affect on trade between Member States – it is sufficient to show that the measure is *capable* of such an effect. This is a particularly all-encompassing interpretation, allowing Member States very little scope in their trading rules.

The 'Rule of Reason'

In Case 120/78, *Rewe-Zentral v Bundesmonopolverwaltung fur Branntwein*, the *Cassis de Dijon* case, the ECJ qualified the above approach by applying 'the Rule of Reason'. The Court held that, in the absence of Community harmonisation rules, where the measure in question is an IDAM (that is, non-discriminatory), it may be *justified* and therefore *not* come within the scope of Art 28 of the EC Treaty provided that is:

(a) 'necessary', in order to satisfy (that is, a measure will be considered 'necessary' if its aim cannot be achieved through less restrictive means);

(b) 'mandatory' requirements.

The Court went on to list particular areas where this may occur, in particular:

- the effectiveness of fiscal supervision;
- the protection of public health;
- the fairness of commercial transactions;
- consumer protection.

This list is not, however, exhaustive and the ECJ has shown itself willing to extend the areas to include the promotion of national culture (Cases 60 and 61/84, *Cinetheque v Federation des Cinemas Francais*) and protection of the environment (Case 302/86, *Commission v Denmark*, the *Danish Bottles* case).

Prior to the introduction of the 'rule of reason' in *Cassis de Dijon*, it was thought that all measures caught within the '*Dassonville* formula' would be prohibited by Art 28 *unless* they could be justified under Art 30 of the EC

Treaty (discussed below). Following *Cassis*, it could be concluded that IDAMs may escape Art 28 of the EC Treaty, provided they can fulfil the necessary criteria as set out above. The approach taken in *Cassis* was confirmed in the Case 788/79, *Italian State v Gilli and Andres*, the *Italian Vinegar* case.

Later re-examination and clarification of the case law by the ECJ

In Cases C-267 and 268/91, *Keck and Mithouard*, the Court took the opportunity to '*re-examine and clarify*' its case law relating to MHEEs.

The Court held that 'contrary to what has previously been decided ... certain selling arrangements' are outside the scope of the *Dassonville* formula, provided that 'those provisions apply to all affected traders operating within the national territory and provided they affect in the same manner, in law and in fact, the marketing of domestic products and those from other Member States'.

While the Court's judgment was intended to clarify the law it has, in reality caused some confusion, particularly with regard to:

• which 'selling arrangements' are now outside the scope of *Dassonville*; and

• which past decisions are overruled by *Keck*.

The Court's judgment, *which clearly relates only to IDAMs*, appears to distinguish between measures which relate to the goods themselves – that is, their intrinsic qualities such as composition, size, labelling, packaging, weight, form, etc – and measures which relate to 'selling arrangements' – that is extrinsic matters such as the marketing of the goods. The Court appears to provide that measures relating to intrinsic qualities come within the scope of Art 28 of the EC Treaty while those relating to 'selling arrangements' do not.

Later decisions of the ECJ appear to support this conclusion. In Cases C-401 and 402/92, *Tankstation't vof* and *Boermans*, for example, the Court held a rule prohibiting the advertising of certain pharmaceutical products to be a 'selling arrangement' which was, as such, not prohibited by Art 28 of the EC Treaty. Similarly, in Case C-292/92, *Hunermund*, the Court also considered a rule relating the compulsory closing times of petrol stations to be a 'selling arrangement' and consequently outside the scope of Art 28.

The present state of affairs

As can be gleaned from the above discussions, the extent of the rules contained within Art 28 of the EC Treaty is still far from certain. It would appear however, that when considering whether a 'measure' comes within the scope of Art 28 of the EC Treaty, one should consider:

- whether or not the measure is distinctly applicable (that is, discriminatory);
- whether it is a 'selling arrangement' which relates to intrinsic or extrinsic characteristics of the goods and, finally;
- whether it can be saved by the 'Rule of Reason'.

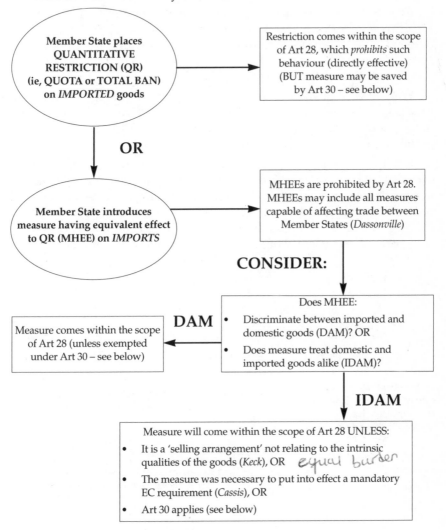

The Prohibition of Quantitative Restrictions and Measures having Equivalent Effect on IMPORTS

MHEEs and exports (Art 29 of the EC Treaty)

There may be instances, although less frequent than in relation to imports, where a Member State may wish to restrict the free flow of exports and consequently the Community has responded to such a possibility.

Article 29 of the EC Treaty prohibits quantitative restrictions and all MHEEs, on imported goods. While the prohibition contained within Art 29 of the EC Treaty appears to mirror that contained within Art 28 of the EC Treaty, this is *not* the case, as ECJ decisions such as *Dassonville*, *Cassis* and *Keck* do not apply to the application of Art 29.

While Art 28 of the EC Treaty has been held to prohibit both DAMs (discriminatory measures) and IDAMS (measures which treat domestic and other goods alike), it would appear that Art 29 of the EC Treaty only prohibits measures which discriminate (DAMs) (Case 15/79, *Groenveld*).

Examples of measures that have been held to be MHEEs with regard to exports include Case 237/82, *Jongeneel Kaas v Netherland*, where inspection documents were required for exports while no such requirement was placed on goods destined for the domestic market, and Case C-5/94, *R v MAFF ex p Lomas*, where national authorities refused to sanction the export of live animals to States where slaughterhouse standards were not thought to be adequate.

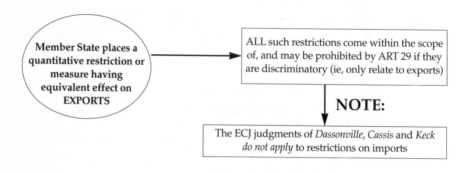

Member State places a quantitative restriction or measure having equivalent effect on EXPORTS

ALL such restrictions come within the scope of, and may be prohibited by ART 29 if they are discriminatory (ie, only relate to exports)

NOTE:

The ECJ judgments of *Dassonville*, *Cassis* and *Keck* *do not apply* to restrictions on imports

Quantitative Restrictions and MHEEs on EXPORTS

Justifying quantitative restrictions and MHEEs (Art 30 of the EC Treaty)

What the Treaty says

The Community has recognised that certain measures put into effect by Member States, although detrimental to free movement of goods, may be necessary to fulfil an important function. In order to give effect to the recognition that the positive affects of certain measures outweigh the negative affects on trade, Art 30 of the EC Treaty provides that: *'The provisions of Arts 28 and 29 shall not preclude prohibitions or restrictions on imports, exports or goods in transit justified on grounds of'*:

- public morality;
- public security or policy;
- protection of the health and life of humans, animals or plants;
- protection of national treasures;
- protection of industrial and commercial property.

The Article goes on to qualify this, providing that: 'Such prohibitions or restrictions shall not, however, constitute a means of arbitrary discrimination or a disguised restriction on trade between member States.'

The jurisprudence of the ECJ

As touched upon earlier, the ECJ has adopted a narrow stance with regard to its interpretation of the measures which may enjoy a derogation under Art 30 of the EC Treaty, as to do otherwise could constitute a threat to the Community's fundamental principle of free trade.

Considering, first, the qualifications added as a rider to Art 30 of the EC Treaty, the Court's attitude is best discovered by consideration of some of its decisions.

'Arbitrary discrimination'

In Case 152/78, *Commission v France*, French advertising restrictions appeared to be biased against grain based spirits, while favouring fruit based spirits. The French authorities attempted to justify this on the grounds of 'public health', arguing that grain based spirits were more likely to be injurious to health. Independent evidence however showed that the effect on health of both spirits to be identical. Interestingly, the French produce fruit based spirits, while grain based spirits are generally imported.

The Court, in its judgment, considered the restriction to be capricious, constituting *arbitrary discrimination*.

'Disguised restriction on trade'

In Case 40/82, *Commission v UK*, the *Newcastle Disease* case, the UK banned the import of poultry and poultry products from countries which did not have a policy of slaughtering birds with Newcastle disease. The UK attempted to justify this on the grounds of 'public health'. Evidence showed that other methods of controlling the disease were equally effective and that the ban had been imposed following pressure from UK poultry producers relating to an increase of turkeys imported from France. Furthermore, when French importers complied with UK requirements, additional restrictions were imposed. The ECJ concluded that the UK's restrictions amounted to a disguised restriction on trade.

The requirement of 'proportionality'

Although not specifically mentioned in Art 30 of the EC Treaty, it is implicit that the general principle of proportionality may apply to any measure for which a Member State is claiming justification. The principle requires that measures be no more than strictly necessary to achieving a particular aim (Case 124/81, *Commission v UK, Re UHT Milk*).

The grounds for justification

The Treaty provides a *closed* list of grounds under which measures may be considered to be justifiable. The Court has expressed unwillingness to consider any new grounds and has refused to accept that measures which seek to ensure consumer protection and protection of the environment, amongst others, could be valid grounds. (See, for example, Case 113/80, *Commission v Ireland*, the *Irish Souvenirs* case.)

(i)   Public morality

Consideration of Case 34/79, *R v Henn and Darby* and Case 121/85, *Conegate Ltd v Customs & Excise*, which are the main authorities in this area, provide examples of the Court's interpretation of this ground.

In *Henn and Darby*, the defendants were accused by UK authorities of illegally importing pornographic material. They argued, in their defence, that UK rules contravened Art 28 of the EC Treaty. The ECJ found that the UK's ban on pornography was justified under Art 30 of the EC Treaty, as it is for each Member State to determine the standards of public morality which exist within its own territory.

In *Conegate*, the defendants imported inflatable, life size 'love dolls' into the UK. The dolls were seized and, once more, it was argued that the UK rules constituted a threat to trade. As UK rules did not contain a similar ban on the domestic manufacture of 'love dolls' and although the Court repeated its *dicta* from *Henn and Darby*, it was held that a Member State may not rely on Art 30 of the EC Treaty *'when its legislation contains no prohibition on the manufacture or marketing of the same goods in its territory'*.

What can be concluded from these decisions is that while the Member States are free to determine moral standards within their own States, they must not place any stricter a burden on non-domestic goods than they do on nationally produced goods.

(ii)   Public policy

Case 7/78, *R v Thompson and Others* – a rare example of a successful action under this ground – involved the right to mint (and melt down) coinage. The Court held that this ground could be successful where *there is a need to protect a right which is traditionally regarded as involving a fundamental interest of the State.*

(iii)   Public security

This ground often goes hand in hand with a claim based on public policy. In Case 72/83, *Campus Oil Ltd v Minister for Industry and Energy*, importers of petroleum products were required to buy 35% of their oil from the Irish National Petroleum Company, at a fixed price. The ECJ accepted that this was to enable the Irish Government to maintain a viable refinery that could meet essential needs in times of crisis and that the national measure could be justified as in the interests of public security.

(iv)   Protection of health and life of humans, animals or plants

The ECJ has made it clear that, when considering whether or not a measure may be justified under this ground, there are a number of issues which may be relevant to its deliberations. These have been held to include:

(a) *the presence, or otherwise, of harmonising legislation.* In the absence of harmonising legislation, the principle of 'mutual recognition' may be relevant. This principle is discussed in further detail below but, briefly, it provides that goods lawfully produced in one Member State should be assumed to reach the minimum requires standards in all Member States (see, also, Case 190/87, *Oberkreisdirektor v Moorman*);

(b) *The state of scientific knowledge* (Case 174/82, *Officier van Justitie v Sandoz* and Case 178/84, *Commission v Germany*, the *German Beer* case). This should be followed but, where it is undecided, the Member State will be provided with a degree of discretion, bearing in mind;

- *the principle of proportionality* (*Sandoz* and the *UHT Milk* case);

- *the existence of a technical need* (see the *German Beer* case). This is often particularly relevant with regard to rules relating to additives;

- *the true need for inspections/spot checks* (again, the 'the rule of mutual recognition' may be relevant). In Case 4/75, *Rewe-Zentralfinanz v Landschwirtschaftskammer, San Jose Scale*, it was held that inspections will only be justified if imported products constitute a real risk not present in comparable domestic goods while, in Case 228/91, *Commission v Italy*, the Court provided that where health certificates are available, spot checks, rather than continual inspection, will be judged as necessary on imports.

It should be evident that an overlap exists between measures justifiable under 'the rule of reason' (*Cassis*) and Art 30 of the EC Treaty, particularly in the area of 'public health'. However, when Member States have previously sought to justify measures on public health grounds, the Court has chosen to consider such requests under Art 30 of the EC Treaty.

(v) Protection of national treasures

There is a paucity of definitive case law in this area and therefore little guidance as to what will be considered to be a 'national treasure'. In the *1st Art Treasures* case, which was brought as a result of Italy's breach of Art 25 of the EC Treaty, the ECJ failed to allow the Italian Government to levy an export tax on 'cultural artifacts' in an attempt to restrict their removal abroad. While Italy's actions were prohibited, the Court's judgment added little to academic understanding in relation to this ground.

(vi) Protection of industrial or commercial property

Industrial or commercial property (or 'intellectual property') rights may take the form of trademarks, copyright, patents, etc.

Protection of such rights encourages innovation and their ownership is complemented by Art 295 of the EC Treaty, which provides: 'The Treaty shall in no way prejudice the rules in Member States governing the system of property ownership.'

Where national rules allow such rights to be protected, an individual with an intellectual property right (IPR) can often rely on such legislation to prevent re-importation of particular goods. National legislation relating to IPR may, however, have the result of restricting trade which is, of course, prohibited under Community law.

The ECJ has struck a balance between the necessary protection of IPR and the principle of free movement of goods by distinguishing between: (1) the existence; and (2) the exercise of such rights.

The Court has provided that IPR will be protected by Art 30 of the EC Treaty only when rights have not been exhausted by the subject matter of the right being put into free circulation within the Community (Case 15/74, *Centrafarm v Sterling Drug*).

Example

Allan has patented a new invention and so an IPR is in *existence*. Should Allan decide to award a license to a manufacturer, Brian, giving Brian the right to produce the invention, Allan will have *exercised* his IP rights.

If the product remains within the Member State, the rights afforded by the award of a patent will be subject to the intellectual property laws *of that Member State only* and Community rules will be irrelevant.

If, however, the product is exported by Brian, Allan will not be able to exert any further control over the product, even if it is re-imported, as the Community will recognise that his rights have been *exhausted* or 'used up' when he awarded Brian authority over the product.

The doctrine of exhaustion of rights has been held to be applicable to:

- patents – Case 15/74, *Centrafarm v Sterling Drug*;
- trade marks – Case 16/74, *Centrafarm v Winthrop*;
- copyright – Case 78/70, *Deutsche Grammophon v Metro*.

It should be noted that a certain amount of secondary legislation has also been issued by the Community with the aim of harmonising the rules in this area.

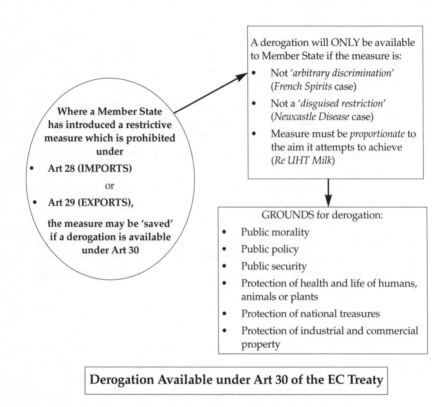

A derogation will ONLY be available to Member State if the measure is:

- Not *'arbitrary discrimination'* (*French Spirits* case)
- Not a *'disguised restriction'* (*Newcastle Disease* case)
- Measure must be *proportionate* to the aim it attempts to achieve (*Re UHT Milk*)

Where a Member State has introduced a restrictive measure which is prohibited under

- **Art 28 (IMPORTS)**

or

- **Art 29 (EXPORTS)**,

the measure may be 'saved' if a derogation is available under Art 30

GROUNDS for derogation:

- Public morality
- Public policy
- Public security
- Protection of health and life of humans, animals or plants
- Protection of national treasures
- Protection of industrial and commercial property

Derogation Available under Art 30 of the EC Treaty

Non-pecuniary barriers to trade and harmonisation of trading rules

The principle of mutual recognition

In the *Cassis* case, the ECJ developed a highly important principle. The Court provided that there is a presumption that goods which have been lawfully produced and marketed in one Member State will comply with the minimum requirements of the importing Member State (this has become known as the principle of mutual recognition).

The Court's approach assumes that all Member States have a broadly equivalent standards when it comes to issues such as health and safety and that all manufacturers will conform to those standards. The presumption can however be *rebutted* by evidence that further measures are necessary to ensure adequate standards are met (Case 18/84, *Commission v France*). This approach should, therefore, always be followed when considering whether measures taken by Member States are indeed 'necessary'.

The principle has also been important to the process of harmonisation of trading rules within the Community. In order to create an integrated market, the Community recognises that trading rules within the of the EC Treaty must be harmonised. The Treaty consequently provides for the harmonisation of national laws via Arts 94 and 95 of the EC Treaty.

Community harmonisation initiatives have, traditionally, been exceedingly detailed and consequently difficult to implement. In recognition of the importance of this principle, the Commission have provided that: '*Any product imported from another Member State must in principle be admitted to the territory of the importing Member State if it has been lawfully produced, that is conforms to rules and processes of manufacture that are customarily and traditionally accepted in the exporting country, and is marketed in the territory of another.*' (Commission Communication OJ 1980 256/2.)

Following the development of the principle of mutual recognition, there has been a 'new approach' to harmonising legislation, with such legislation now needing to define no more than the essential health and safety requirements of a product.

Students who have made it this far will probably agree with a comment made at the beginning of the chapter, that is, the rules relating to the free movement of goods are complex! In recognition of this fact, a flow chart is provided below in order to assist students navigate the shark infested waters often encountered when attempting to answer questions in this area.

The prohibition of charges and measures imposed by Member States capable of having an effect on the free movement of goods within the Community

Has a MEMBER STATE put into effect a restriction/measure which is:

- A *PECUNIARY* barrier to trade (customs duty, charge having equivalent effect or discriminatory internal taxation)

AND/OR*

- A *NON-PECUNIARY* barrier to trade (quantitative restriction or measure having equivalent effect)?

PECUNIARY barriers include:

- New customs duties – prohibited by Art 25

- *CHEEs* – prohibited by Art 25 *BUT* a charge for an inspection OR a fee for service will not be considered a CHEE (if the necessary criteria can be fulfilled)

- *Discriminatory internal taxation* prohibited by Art 90 (both direct and indirectly discriminatory charges are prohibited)

NON-PECUNIARY barriers include:

- Quantitative restrictions and MHEEs on IMPORTS, prohibited by Art 28

  (BUT consider what comes within the definition of a MHEE – consider, particularly *Keck* with regard to 'selling arrangements' which are outside Art 28)

- Quantitative restrictions and MHEEs on EXPORTS, prohibited by Art 29

UNLESS: The restriction or measure can be 'saved' by Art 30
(Note: MHEEs on IMPORTS may also be 'justified' under the 'rule of reason' but only if they are non-discriminatory)

---

*Take care – if a *charge* is levied for an *inspection* you will need to consider both pecuniary (the charge) and quantitative (the inspection) restrictions

8 Free Movement of Persons

As already considered, the creation of a common market is a primary aim of the EC. In order to ensure that this aim is achieved, the EC Treaty provides that all obstacles to free movement of goods, persons, services and capital shall be abolished within the Community.

The free movement of persons is considered to be fundamental to the creation of the common market. Without a mobile workforce, British workers, for example, would not be able to enter Germany to provide their expertise should a manpower or skills shortage exist, neither would a Belgian entrepreneur be able expand his business into France, nor a Swedish physiotherapist be able to cross the border into Denmark to provide his occasional services to a client with back problems.

The consequences of all of these occurrences is likely to be detrimental to the creation of an integrated Community and so the Treaty gives rights to all of these persons to work, set up a business or provide a service throughout the EC. The provision of the right to free movement within the Community does not, of course, only have economic implications and the social aspects of such a right are also important.

THE IMPORTANCE OF NATIONALITY

It is important to be clear at the outset that rights relating to free movement are restricted to nationals of the Member States and citizens of non-Member States are not directly provided with such rights.

AN OVERVIEW OF THE TREATY PROVISIONS RELATING TO FREE MOVEMENT OF PERSONS

The Treaty provides Member States with a number of *obligations* relating to the treatment of nationals who wish to move from State to State within the

Community. Conversely, the Treaty also provides citizens with *rights* that are to be enjoyed in relation to free movement.

The Treaty differentiates between *workers* (or employees), those wishing to *establish* a business and those wishing to provide (or receive) a *service*:

- Arts 39–42 of the EC Treaty relate to the rights of wage and salary earners to travel to and take up employment in a host State;
- Arts 43–48 of the EC Treaty relate to the rights of the self-employed, companies and firms to establish a permanent base in another Member State;
- Arts 49–55 of the EC Treaty afford rights to individuals to cross a frontier in order to provide or receive services without establishing a base in another Member State.

The Treaty does, however, place limits on such rights and Member States are allowed to derogate from their obligations in certain, defined circumstances, which are discussed below.

In addition to the provision of the above rights, which are afforded to specific categories of person, the Treaty contains certain, less specific, provisions which nevertheless underpin the free movement of persons. These include:

- Art 12 of the EC Treaty, which provides a general prohibition on discrimination on the grounds of nationality;
- Art 17 of the EC Treaty, which provides that each person holding the nationality of a Member State shall be a citizen of the Union.

Categorising 'persons'

Community law provides rights relating to free movement according to the 'category' that a person may fall into. As already touched upon above, *citizenship* of one of the Community's Member States is vital if a person is to enjoy 'independent' rights. ('Dependant' rights may be available to non-nationals provided they form part of the family of an EC citizen. This is discussed in further detail below.)

In addition, it is important to be able initially to distinguish between the following two categories of person:

- non-economically active persons; and
- economically active persons.

Free movement of non-economically active persons

The Treaty does not provide the right of free movement to those who are not economically active. This is understandable, as the activities of the Community are largely economic in nature. However, three directives have been enacted (the '90s Directives') containing provisions which, in effect, allow non-economically active nationals rights relating to free movement:

(i) *Directive 90/366/EEC* (as amended by *Directive (93/96/EEC)*) provides the right of residence to *students*. A residence permit for the student, his spouse and any children will be granted for the duration of the student's course, though it is to be renewed annually and conditional upon the student continuing to hold a place at university/third level educational establishment.

The European Court of Justice (ECJ) has been keen to point out that the rights of students may also be affected by Art 12 of the EC Treaty, which provides protection from discrimination on the grounds of nationality. The imposition of an enrolment fee for a vocational course on non-national students, but not nationals, has been held to breach this Article (Case 293/83, *Gravier v City of Liège*). The definition of 'vocational' is broad and inclusive, and the ECJ have ruled that it may include university courses – other than those intended to improve general knowledge – as well as those which prepare students for an occupation (Case 24/86, *Blaizot v University of Liège*). It would appear, however, that, as yet, there is no requirement that host States allow non-nationals equality of access and other benefits in all areas of education.

(ii) *Directive 90/365/EEC*, which applies to *former* employees and self-employed persons who have ceased their professional activity as a result of *retirement* or *incapacity* and wish to *move* to a host State during their retirement. (The rights of retired or incapacitated workers wishing to *remain* in a host State are considered below.)

(iii)*Directive 90/364/EEC* provides the right of residence to those who do not qualify for it under any other EC provisions. A residence permit will only be granted to those who can demonstrate that they have sufficient resources so not as to be reliant on the social security system of the host State.

Free movement of economically active persons

This group of persons can be further subdivided into:

• employees or workers;

• the self-employed.

This chapter is primarily concerned with the free movement of workers but the rights of the self-employed will be considered, briefly, at the end of the chapter. It may be helpful to understand at the outset that the *aims* of free movement, whether in relation to goods, workers or the self-employed, run parallel and as a result a similar approach is evident throughout all the areas.

OVERVIEW OF FREE MOVEMENT OF PERSONS

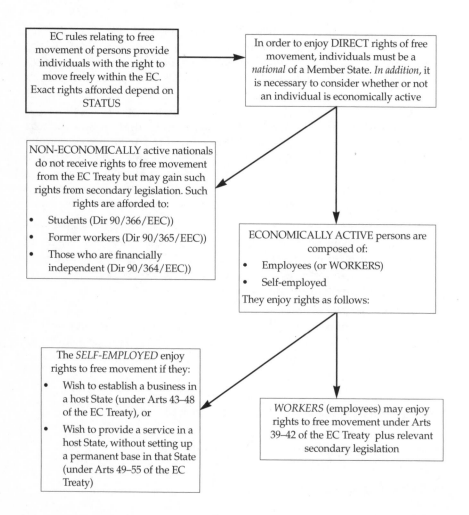

EC rules relating to free movement of persons provide individuals with the right to move freely within the EC. Exact rights afforded depend on STATUS

In order to enjoy DIRECT rights of free movement, individuals must be a *national* of a Member State. *In addition*, it is necessary to consider whether or not an individual is economically active

NON-ECONOMICALLY active nationals do not receive rights to free movement from the EC Treaty but may gain such rights from secondary legislation. Such rights are afforded to:

- Students (Dir 90/366/EEC))
- Former workers (Dir 90/365/EEC))
- Those who are financially independent (Dir 90/364/EEC))

ECONOMICALLY ACTIVE persons are composed of:

- Employees (or WORKERS)
- Self-employed

They enjoy rights as follows:

The *SELF-EMPLOYED* enjoy rights to free movement if they:

- Wish to establish a business in a host State (under Arts 43–48 of the EC Treaty), or
- Wish to provide a service in a host State, without setting up a permanent base in that State (under Arts 49–55 of the EC Treaty)

WORKERS (employees) may enjoy rights to free movement under Arts 39–42 of the EC Treaty plus relevant secondary legislation

(1)   FREE MOVEMENT OF WORKERS

(Articles 39–42 of the EC Treaty)

Community rules relating to the free movement of workers are contained in Arts 39–42 of the EC Treaty. In addition to the rules contained therein, these provisions have been expanded upon by secondary legislation. Both sets of rules have also been the subject of extensive interpretation by the ECJ and each of these sources of Community law will be considered in turn.

(i)   How is the term 'worker' defined?

Neither the Treaty nor secondary legislation provides a definition of the term 'worker'. This has been left to the ECJ who have made it clear that, as it is a Community concept, they alone can define it. While case law makes it clear that 'worker' generally refers to an *employed* person, the term has been interpreted very widely, allowing as many people as possible to enjoy the rights provided, thus, promoting free movement.

The following decisions provide a flavour of the Court's broad and inclusive attitude as to who will come within its definition of the term:

*   Case 75/63, *Hoekstra (née Unger) v BBDA*: a worker who had *lost his job* but was capable of finding another should be considered a worker;
*   Case 53/81, *Levin v Staatssecretaris*: a *part time* employee is to be considered a worker, provided the work is *'real' or genuine work* of an *economic* nature and not nominal or minimal;
*   Case 139/85, *Kempf v Staatssecretaris van Justitie*: a part time music teacher (from Germany) even though in receipt of *supplementary benefit* (in the Netherlands) to bring his wage up to minimum levels, came within the term;
*   Case 196/87, *Steymann v Staatssecretaris van Justitie*: a member of a religious community provided with his 'keep' and *pocket money,* but not formal wages, was held to be a worker;
*   Case 344/87, *Bettray v Staatssecretaris van Justitie*: an important case demonstrating the *limits of the term* worker. It was held that, as the position was artificially created by the government as part of a drug rehabilitation programme, he could not be considered to be engaged in 'economic activity' or a 'genuine' nature.

(ii) Rights of exit, entry and residence afforded to workers

What does the Treaty say?

Article 39 of the EC Treaty contains the principal provisions relating to migrant *workers*. These include:

- the right to accept offers of employment actually made and to move freely within the host State for this purpose;
- the right to reside in the host State, for the purpose of employment, under the same rules as enjoyed by nationals;
- the right to remain in the host State after having been employed in that State (following retirement or incapacity).

What does secondary legislation say?

Rights provided under the Treaty have been extended and expanded upon by secondary legislation (passed under the authority of Art 40 of the EC Treaty – the legal base). Directive 68/360/EEC relates to rights concerned with exiting a home State, entering a host State and also applying for a residence permit.

The Directive provides detailed rules as to the documents required when leaving one Member State and entering another. In order to ensure that a home State cannot deny exit to key workers, the Directive provides that 'exit' States must provide their citizens with a passport and allow them to leave.

It further provides that the 'entrance' State cannot demand entry visas or other such documents from EC nationals, although a passport or identity card may be required. Any worker who provides such documentation, plus proof of employment, must be granted a residence permit expediently, valid for at least five years and automatically renewable.

What does the ECJ say?

Neither Art 39 nor Directive 68/360/EEC make any reference to the right to move freely in *search* of employment. The ECJ has, however, held that an individual with a genuine chance of finding work must be allowed to enter and remain for a *reasonable* amount of time while seeking work (Case C-292/89, *R v Immigration Appeal Tribunal ex p Antonissen*). The rights of those searching for work do not extend to the issue of a residency permit.

Can these rights be lost?

Restrictions on exit, entry and residence

The Community recognises that there are certain circumstances under which it is neither reasonable nor desirable to allow workers the right to move freely around the Community. Community law therefore allows Member States to invoke exceptions to the rule of free movement as follows.

The Treaty

Article 39(3) of the EC Treaty provides that Member States may deny workers the right of free movement where it can be justified on the grounds of public policy, public security or public health. (It should be noted that the grounds of public policy and public security overlap to such an extent that they can, in practice, be regarded as a single category).

Secondary legislation

The derogation provided in Art 39 of the EC Treaty is repeated and expanded upon by Directives 68/360/EEC and 64/221/EEC. Directive 64/221/EEC provides that measures taken on the basis of public policy or security must be based exclusively on the *personal conduct* of the individual concerned (see Case 41/74, *Van Duyn v Home Office*).

The Directive also provides that the existence of previous criminal convictions will *not automatically* allow a Member State to deny a worker his rights of entry and residence and neither will the expiry of a passport or identity card justify expulsion.

The Annex to the Directive provides a list of diseases which will allow a Member State to deny entry, but any disease or disability contracted *after* entry may not result in expulsion or denial of the renewal of a residence permit. The Annex also provides that drug addiction or mental disturbance may also constitute a threat to public policy or public security.

Importantly, Directive 64/221/EEC also provides procedural safeguards that must be followed should a worker's right to entry and/or residence be denied. The Directive, which takes its example from continental administrative law, provides:

- the right to be given detailed *reasons* for the refusal of a residence permit or deportation (unless security is at stake);
- the right of *appeal* from any such decisions (the appeal body must be independent from that which made the initial decision);
- the right to *judicial review* of the decision.

THE APPROACH OF THE ECJ

The ECJ has taken a narrow approach to the interpretation of the legislation restricting the free movement of workers. As with the exceptions to the rules governing free movement of goods (Art 30 of the EC Treaty), exceptions to the free movement of workers must be *proportionate* and *objectively justifiable*. This can be evidenced by consideration of the following decisions of the ECJ.

The ECJ provided in Case 36/75, *Rutili v Ministre de l'Interieur*, that a Member State claiming a derogation on the grounds of public policy and/or security may only be denied his rights if his presence would constitute a *'genuine and sufficiently serious threat to public policy'*. This was extended in Case 30/77, *R v Bouchereau*, where the Court provided that the threat must also *'affect one of the fundamental interests of the State'*.

In Cases 115 and 116/81, *Adoui and Cornuaille v Belgian State*, the *French Prostitutes* case, the ECJ held that the public policy justification does not allow expulsion where similar conduct by nationals does not incur a proportionately restrictive sanction. (In this case, French nationals were denied entry to Belgium due to their 'moral standards', despite the fact that prostitution is not illegal there – an obvious example of discrimination against migrants.)

Previous (and even current) *criminal convictions* do not necessarily provide grounds for exclusion on public policy grounds unless they provide evidence of a *present* threat to public policy, as can be demonstrated by the following cases:

- in Case 30/77, *R v Bouchereau*, B, a French national, came to work in the UK in 1975. He was convicted of unlawful possession of drugs in June 1976, having pleaded guilty to a similar offence in January 1976 (for which he received a 12 month conditional discharge). The magistrates' court referred to the ECJ questions to determine to what extent previous convictions may be considered as a ground for exclusion.

The ECJ held that previous criminal conviction may only be taken into account as evidence of personal conduct where it constitutes a present threat to the requirements of public policy, by indicating a likelihood of recurrence. Past conduct alone, however, may be sufficient to constitute a present threat where the conduct is sufficiently serious.

- in Case 67/74, *Bonsignore v Oberstadtdirektor of the City of Cologne*, B, an Italian working in Germany, accidentally shot his brother with a pistol. He was convicted and fined for unlawful possession of a firearm and was ordered to be deported. He challenged the deportation order in the

German courts that referred to the ECJ the question of whether deportation may be justified on public policy grounds as *a general preventative measure to deter others.*

The ECJ held that the public policy requirement may only be invoked to justify a deportation for breaches of the peace and public security which may be committed by the individual concerned and *not* for reasons of a general preventive nature.

(iii) The right to be treated equally with domestic workers

What does the Treaty say?

Article 39 of the EC Treaty provides that migrant workers must not be discriminated against on the basis of their nationality with regards to employment, remuneration and other conditions of work and employment.

Article 12 of the EC Treaty also provides a more general right not to be discriminated against on the basis of nationality.

What does secondary legislation say?

Council Regulation (EEC) 1612/68 expands upon rights provided by the Treaty with regard to access to, and conditions of, employment. In addition, the Regulation provides that migrant workers must be provided with the same *social and tax advantages* as national workers and any rule which makes it more difficult for a migrant worker to find work, etc, in another Member State is, *prima facie,* contrary to Community law.

All discriminatory rules, whether administrative, created by legislation, or merely accepted practice (and including those made by autonomous professional bodies) are prohibited.

Under Regulation (EEC) 1612/68, migrant workers must have the same priority, employment law, conditions of work, and protection as 'domestic' workers. Both direct and indirect (or covert) discrimination is prohibited and the following areas are highlighted by the legislation:

(i) *trade union membership* – a migrant worker retains equality as to trade union membership and office;

(ii) *housing* – a migrant worker must have the same rights as a domestic worker in relation to housing, including, for example, property ownership;

(iii) *access to training* – migrant workers must be allowed access to *vocational* training at vocational schools and retraining centres under the same conditions as national workers. 'Vocational schools' have been interpreted as meaning institutions which give sandwich or apprenticeship courses, as opposed to those offering purely academic courses;

(iv) *social advantages not related directly to employment* – Regulation (EEC) 1612/68 provides that migrant workers are entitled to the same social advantages as national workers. It has been held that such advantages need not be attached to a contract of employment, and that they continue after the worker's death to benefit the family remaining;

(v) *tax advantages* – migrant workers are entitled to the same tax advantages as nationals of the Member State. However, a residence requirement that is indirectly discriminatory may be *objectively justified* where the situation of the national worker and the migrant worker is not comparable.

THE ECJ

The Court has been called upon to clarify the situation with regard to access to education and training on a number of occasions, particularly in regard to the provision of maintenance grants.

In Case 39/86, *Lair v Universität-Hanover*, the Court explained that while migrant workers may be entitled to grants providing access to education (that is, tuition fees) in the same way as domestic workers, the same cannot be said of maintenance grants which need only be made available if the course is vocational. This view was upheld in Case 197/86, *Brown v Secretary of State for Scotland*.

The Court has provided that a migrant worker's right to claim the same social advantages as nationals has come to depend not so much on the claimant's status as a worker, but on his lawful residence in that State (and, as such, will be relevant to *all persons*, not only workers, enjoying rights of free movement). In Case 32/75, *Fiorini v SNCF*, for example, the Court held that social and tax advantages are not reliant on a contract of employment being in existence. In this case, the widow of a migrant worker, entitled to remain in the host State, was entitled to all such advantages enjoyed by the widow of a domestic worker.

(iv) Exceptions to the principle of equal rights for migrant workers

Social advantages

As already touched upon above, eligibility for educational grants may be limited, while an important limitation was imposed on the right to claim equal social advantages in Case 316/85, *Centre Public de l'Aide Social de Courcelles v Lebon*. In this case, it was held that equality of treatment in respect of all social advantages was only available to persons entitled to residence by reason of employment, and not to persons permitted temporary rights of residence in order to *search* for work.

As discussed above, indirectly discriminatory tax rules may be objectively justified by a Member State (see Case 279/93, *Schumacker*, and Case 204/90, *Bachmann*), while an important limitation to equal access to employment relates to linguistic ability.

Linguistic knowledge

Regulation (EEC) 1612/68 permits the imposition on non-nationals of conditions relating to *linguistic knowledge* required by reason of the nature of the post to be filled. It should be noted, however, that any State policy regarding linguistic knowledge must not be disproportionate to the aim to be achieved, neither should the manner in which it is applied discriminate against nationals of other Member States.

In Case 379/87, *Groener v Minister of Education*, for example, a Dutch national was not appointed to a teaching post at an Irish college when she failed an oral test. The test, which related to her competency in Gaelic, applied to both nationals and migrant workers alike, had been introduced to encourage the use of the language. The Court concluded that the Irish State was within its rights to implement such a State policy, provided that the requirement was not disproportionate to the aim.

In reality, the variety of languages spoken within the Community undoubtedly has an adverse affect on cross-border mobility. Tethered largely by linguistic differences, it is interesting to note that less than 1% of EU citizens live outside their country of origin.

(v) The 'public service' exception to free movement (Art 39(4) of the EC Treaty)

Article 39(4) of the EC Treaty permits Member States to deny or restrict free movement to migrant workers on the basis that they wish to take up employment in the 'public service'.

The exact scope of 'pubic service' is not defined by the legislation and, not surprisingly, as it provides an exception to the fundamental Community principle of free movement, has been narrowly interpreted by the ECJ. The Court has shed considerable light on the extent and application of the rule and the following cases are particularly enlightening.

First, the Court has held that the Art 39(4) of the EC Treaty cannot be invoked by Member States in relation to terms and conditions of employment and applies only to *access* to employment (Case 152/73, *Sotgui v Deutsche Bundespost*).

In Case 149/79, *Commission v Belgium (Re Public Employees)*, Belgian law reserving posts in the public service for Belgian nationals, *irrespective of the duties performed*, was found to come outside the scope of the Art 39(4) of the EC Treaty defence. To come within the ambit of Art 39(4), the Court held that employment must involve *'direct or indirect participation in the exercise of powers conferred by public law and duties designed to safeguard the general interests of the State or other public authorities'*.

The implication of this and other supporting decisions, is that only high level posts in which the post-holder owes a particular allegiance to the State may be covered (for example, the armed forces, police, judiciary, tax authorities and high-ranking civil servants, etc). This view is reinforced by the Notice in 1988 (OJ No 72/2) in which the Commission provided some guidance as to which post would be covered. The Commission concluded that the following would be unlikely to be:

- public health services;
- teaching in State educational establishments;
- research for non-military purposes in public establishments;
- public bodies responsible for administering commercial services.

In view of the Court's restrictive attitude and the Commission guidance, this has remained a contentious area. While the EC recognises a need for Member States to preserve their own national identity, the Community has not been prepared to allow them to do this to the detriment of free movement.

(vi) The right of migrant workers to remain after employment has ceased (Art 39(3)(d) of the EC Treaty)

Article 39(3)(d) of the EC Treaty provides workers with the right to remain in a host State after being employed in that State.

The Treaty Article anticipates the enactment of secondary legislation and the right of a worker to remain in a host Member State on retirement or where he/she ceases to be employed as a result of permanent incapacity, has been expanded upon by Commission Regulation (EEC) 1251/70.

Retirement

Under the Regulation, a worker acquires a right of residence on retirement where:

- he has reached the age laid down by the law of the host State for entitlement to an old age pension; *and*
- he has been employed in the host State for at least 12 months; *and*
- he has resided in the host State for a minimum of three years.

Incapacity

Under the Regulation a worker acquires the right to remain in a host State upon incapacity where:

- he has resided continuously in the host State for more than two years; and
- he ceases to work there as an employed person as the result of *permanent* incapacity; or
- the worker is incapacitated as the result of an accident at work or an occupational disease which entitles him to a pension for which an institution of that State is wholly or partly responsible.

It should be noted that the conditions as to length of residency, in relation to both retirement and incapacity, *will not apply* if the worker's spouse is a national of the worker's host Member State.

Workers who live in one host State but work in another

Certain workers may find themselves working in one host State while residing in another. Providing such workers can demonstrate:

- three years' continuous residence and employment in the territory of a host State where they wish to remain; and
- they return at least once a week to that State,

they will have the right to remain in the State in which they are domiciled after ceasing work in the second host State.

The right to a residence permit and social advantages after retirement or incapacity

Persons exercising their right to remain after retirement or incapacity will be entitled to a residence permit which must be valid throughout the territory of the State concerned and automatically renewable. They may also claim all the social advantages provided by that State on the same basis as nationals.

(vii)   Rights relating to workers' families

Primary legislation does not directly refer to a migrant worker's right to be joined by his family, nor does it specify what entitlements family members may enjoy in a host State. This has been left to secondary legislation.

Regulation (EEC) 1612/68 provides certain rights in relation to workers' families. The Regulation, for example, provides that rights relating to a worker's family are *not* dependent upon the family members being citizens of a Member State and family members may consequently enjoy rights despite being non-EU citizens.

There is however, a requirement that the worker have adequate housing available when his/her family arrives. This has been confirmed by the ECJ in Case 131/85, *Gul*, but the Court has also explained that there is no requirement that the family member(s) *continue* to live with the worker (Case 267/83, *Diatta v Land Berlin*) for any set period.

The composition of a worker's 'family'

Regulation (EEC) 1612/68 provides that a worker's 'family' may consist of:
- the *spouse* of worker;
- children, grandchildren and other *descendants*, provided that they are under 21 and/or dependent;
- parents, grandparents and other *ascendants*, provided they are dependent.

The term 'spouse' has been interpreted by the Court to relate to legally married persons only (Case 59/85, *Netherlands v Reed*). However, the Court went on to explain that in a Member State where a stable relationship enjoyed by an unmarried couple is accorded similar status to marriage, this will be considered to be a 'social advantage'. To treat such couples differently would consequently amount to discrimination on the grounds of nationality.

The Court has not specifically dealt with the issue of divorce, but in Case C-370/90 *R v Immigration Appeal Tribunal ex p Secretary of State for the Home Department*, the *Singh* case, the ECJ held that the presence of a *decree nisi* did not affect the residence rights of the non-EC national spouse.

Rights to be enjoyed by workers' families

Rights of exit, entry and residence

Dependant rights relating to exit, entry and residence are, like those of workers, largely governed by Directive 68/360/EEC, which provides that *'members of the family shall enjoy the same right as the national on whom they are dependent'*. Family members need the same documentation as workers in order to enjoy rights of exit and entry. In order to obtain a residence permit family members must produce documents which demonstrate:

- their identity (a valid passport or identity card);
- their relationship to the worker;
- that they are dependent on the worker.

The right to take up employment

Regulation (EEC) 1612/68 provides workers' families with the right to take up employment in the host State. If the family member is an EU national employment will, of course, give them independent rights and they will no longer have to depend on rights provided via their relationship with the original worker.

The right to education

Under Regulation (EEC) 1612/68, children of a worker residing in a host State enjoy non-discriminatory access to general educational, apprenticeship and vocational training schemes. This has been broadly interpreted by the ECJ who have held that migrant workers children are entitled to exactly the same benefits as children of domestic workers, *including* educational grants (Case 76/72, *Michel S*).

This broad interpretative approach can be evidenced by decisions such as Cases 389 and 380/87, *Echternach and Moritz v Netherlands Ministry for Education and Science*, where the Court held that children of migrant workers could remain in the host State to finish their education, *even when their parents had returned home*. Similarly, in Case C-7/94, *Gaal*, the Court provided that educational rights include the right to complete a course, even after a once dependent child reaches the age of 21 (to act otherwise would discourage integration).

Workers spouses do not enjoy such wide rights in relation to education, but they have been held entitled to equal *access* to educational, apprenticeship or vocational training schemes by reason of non-discrimination provisions enshrined in Art 12 of the EC Treaty (see, for example, Case 152/82, *Forcheri v Belgium*).

Other rights

As has already been established, the rights afforded to workers' families largely flow from their relationship with a migrant worker. It should not be forgotten however, that Art 12 of the EC Treaty provides EU citizens with a general right not to be discriminated against on grounds of their nationality.

More specifically the ECJ have elaborated on the extent of dependent rights in a number of cases, particularly with regard to 'social advantages'. In Case 32/75, *Cristini v SNCF*, the Court held that the term *'cannot be interpreted restrictively'*, as to do so would hamper integration. In this particular case, a French railway company offered large (French) families reduced travel rates. These were denied to the Cristini family on the basis of their nationality (Italian). The French company argued that only social advantages connected to a contract of employment need be provided to non-nationals.

The Court held that this argument was contrary to provisions of Regulation (EEC) 1612/68, which is intended to ensure non-discrimination. The case may be used to argue, by analogy, that behaviour which discriminates against a worker's family legally resident in a host State, on the basis of their nationality, is contrary to Community law.

The right to remain

Regulation (EEC) 1251/70 not only details the rights of workers to remain in a host State, but also provides that members of a worker's family will be permitted to remain if the worker dies during his working life, IF:

- the worker has, on the date of his decease, resided continuously in that State for at least two years; *or*

BASIC RIGHTS:

- Art 39 provides the right to take up offers of work, move freely for this purpose and also to remain after being employed
- Dir (68/360/EEC) expands on this with regard to rights of exit from home State, documents for entry to host State and residency
- ECJ has interpreted such rights widely, eg, the right to free movement in *search* of work is provided (*Antonissen*)

CAN RIGHTS BE DENIED BY THE HOST STATE?:

- Treaty (Art 39(3)) provides Member State may deny rights on grounds of public policy/security/ health
- Dirs (68/360/EEC) and (62/221/EEC) expand upon this, providing procedural safeguards such as right to appeal deportation order
- ECJ have interpreted restrictions narrowly, eg, loss of right must relate to **personal behaviour** (*Van Duyn*) which must be a present and **sufficiently serious threat** (*Rutili*) to **fundamental interests of State** (*Bouchereau*). In addition nationals and migrants must be treated alike (*Adoui*)

The Treaty does not define **'WORKER'** The ECJ has defined the term broadly and inclusively to include anyone who provides work of a real, genuine and economic nature (*Levin*)

Workers' rights to free movement within the EU Arts 39–42

RIGHTS OF WORKERS' FAMILIES:

Workers' families (including those who are non-EC nationals) also enjoy rights to free movement.

- Family members generally include both dependant ascendants and decedents (Reg (EEC) 1612/68, but see, also, *Netherlands v Reed*)
- Rights of exit, entry and residence for families are contained in Dir (68/360/EEC) and are largely as for workers themselves
- Family members may take up employment and enjoy education (cf academic and vocational) and social advantage as for domestic workers dependants (see, also, Art 12)

THE 'PUBLIC SERVICE' exception to the equality rules:

- Art 39(4) provides that the right to employment may be denied to migrant workers wishing to work in the public service
- Once more, ECJ has interpreted restrictions narrowly, eg, *Re Public Employees*
- Commission has taken similar approach – see Notice 1988 (OJ 72/2)

OTHER RIGHTS INCLUDE:

- To be treated equally with domestic workers (Art 39 and Reg (EEC) 1612/68) with regard to work issues and social advantages, etc (linguistic exceptions may exist – Reg (EEC) 1612/68 and *Groener*)
- To remain after retirement due to age or ill health (Art 39 and Reg (EEC) 1251/70)

WORKERS' Rights in Relation to FREE MOVEMENT

- his death resulted from an accident at work or an occupational disease; *or*
- the surviving spouse is a national of the State of residence or would have been if he had not lost that nationality due to marriage to the worker.

If the worker dies after he has retired, provided he had already acquired the right to remain in the host State, his family will continue to enjoy the right to remain after his death.

The ECJ has also confirmed that the surviving family of a deceased worker will also enjoy equality of treatment with nationals by virtue of Regulation (EEC) 1251/70 (*Cristini*).

FREEDOM OF ESTABLISHMENT AND FREEDOM TO PROVIDE SERVICES

Articles 43–48 and 49–55 of the EC Treaty

In addition to promoting free movement of workers and protecting migrant workers and their families from discrimination on grounds of nationality, the Treaty also provides similar rights and protection to the self-employed.

Article 43 of the EC Treaty prohibits restrictions from being placed on those who wish to *establish* a business in a host State, while Art 49 of the EC Treaty affords free movement to those who wish to *provide a service* in a host State, *without setting up a permanent base* in that State.

While the Treaty provides three sets of provisions covering the free movement of the three different groups of economically active persons, the Court has concentrated on emphasising the common ground that exists between them.

In Case 48/75, *Royer*, the Court observed that the free movement of workers, freedom of establishment and freedom to provide services are all *'based on the same principles in so far as they concern the entry into and the residence in the territory of Member States of persons covered by Community law and the prohibition of all discrimination between them on grounds of nationality'.*

It should therefore be borne in mind that the various provisions have much in common, with the boundary between establishment and provision of services being particularly indistinct.

(2) RIGHTS OF ESTABLISHMENT

Basic provisions

Article 43 of the EC Treaty provides EC nationals with the right to establish a business (that is set up a permanent base) in a host State under the same conditions enjoyed by nationals of that State.

This right is also applicable to the setting up of agencies, branches or subsidiaries of businesses that have been established in other States. Both natural and artificial legal persons are provided with rights (see Art 50 of the EC Treaty), as natural person may establish a business, but artificial persons (that is, the already established corporation) may also set up agencies, branches or subsidiaries.

Those carrying out the activities set out above are required to comply with the national laws applicable in the host State *unless those laws discriminate on the basis of nationality*. Such discrimination is prohibited both by Art 43 of the EC Treaty and, in a rather more general manner, by Art 12 of the EC Treaty. Discriminatory rules will therefore conflict with Community law and must consequently be set aside.

What amounts to 'discrimination'?

In line with its case law in the area of free movement of goods, the Court has provided that both *directly and indirectly discriminatory* rules may breach Art 43 of the EC Treaty. While national rules which apply only to establishment by non-nationals are likely to be discriminatory, national laws which appear to apply equally to non-nationals and nationals alike may also breach Art 43 of the EC Treaty (Case 71/76, *Thieffry*). (This can be compared to the manner in which the Court has declared that both distinctly and indistinctly applicable measures may be prohibited under rules relating to the free movement of goods (*Dassonville*).)

In Case 143/87, *Stanton v INASTI*, the Court went even further by providing that any national rule, whether or not discriminatory, which 'might place Community citizens at a disadvantage' may be prohibited unless it can be objectively justified.

The argument behind such a wide definition is that such rules provide an excessive barrier to the achievement of the aim of free movement and it appears evident that the Court now appears to be interpreting rules relating to free movement of goods and free movement of persons in an analogous manner.

Problems associated with qualifications

National requirements relating to qualifications can result in a significant barrier to the free movement of persons. Under Art 47 of the EC Treaty, the Council is provided with the authority to issue directives in regard to recognition of training and qualifications obtained within the Community and as a result a considerable amount of harmonising legislation has been enacted.

In the absence of such legislation, the ECJ has, however, held that national authorities have an obligation to consider the training and/or qualifications held by a non-national and compare them with the domestic provision/requirements. Where they are found to be equivalent, the host State must recognise them as such (Case 340/89, *Vlassopoulou*).

If they are found not to be equivalent, the host State must provide reasons for their decision, which must be open to judicial review. (Case 222/86, *UNECTEF v Heylens*). If qualifications are found to be 'part equivalent' the host State may require further training be undertaken in order to 'make up the difference'.

Rights of entry, residence and equal treatment for the self-employed and their families

Directive 73/148/EEC provides migrants, *and their families*, with the right to enter and reside in a host State for the purpose of establishing a business. The Directive's terms are very similar to those found under Directive 68/360/EEC, which provides workers with their rights of exit, entry and residence.

Migrants wishing to remain in a host State following self-employment are provided with the right to do so under Directive 75/34/EEC, while rights to equal treatment with nationals are provided by Directive 73/148/EEC.

In view of the similarity between the above rules and those relating to workers, an analogous view can be taken with regard to interpretation and application of such rules.

EXCEPTIONS TO THE RIGHT OF FREEDOM OF ESTABLISHMENT

As we have already seen in relation to the free movement of workers, restrictive and/or discriminatory measures may be justified on grounds of public policy, security and health and also with regard to employment in the public sector. *Similar* grounds may also be argued in relation to establishment and the provision of services.

In addition, the Court has provided that 'justification' may also be available along similar lines to those argued in *Cassis de Dijon*, in relation to free movement of goods (see Chapter 7). Each ground is considered in further detail below.

The 'official authority' exception

Article 45 of the EC Treaty provides that the rules concerning freedom of establishment will not apply to those who *'exercise official authority'*.

The exception will be relevant in relation to the exercise of an official (State) power. The ECJ have confirmed that it is to be applied in a similar manner to the exception found under Art 39(4) of the EC Treaty, that is the 'public service' exception to free movement of workers (Case 2/74, *Reyners v Belgium*). As the Court has interpreted the 'public service' exception narrowly (see above), a similar stance could be assumed here.

The 'public policy, public service and public health' exception

Article 46 of the EC Treaty provides for exceptions *'on grounds of public policy, public security or public health'*, which the Court has held should be construed as *per* Art 39(3) of the EC Treaty (Case 36/74, *Walgrave and Koch*) and, indeed, secondary legislation expanding upon this derogation relates to both workers *and* establishment (Directive (64/221/EEC)).

The 'public interest' exception

The EC Treaty (Art 30 of the EC Treaty) provides that certain restrictive measures may be justified in relation the prohibition of quantitative restrictions and measures having equivalent effect on the import and export of goods within the EC (Arts 28 and 29 of the EC Treaty). In addition to these express exceptions, the ECJ also developed the 'Rule of Reason' in *Cassis*, which provided other circumstances in which a restrictive measure could be justified.

The Court has also developed a similar 'rule' with regard to free movement of persons. Although first developed in relation to the provision of services (see judgments such as Case 33/74, *Van Binsbergen*, and Case 279/80, *Webb*), the Court appears to have provided that where a national measure hinders free movement rather than discriminates against non-nationals, that measure may be justified in appropriate circumstances.

In Case C-55/94, *Gebhard*, the ECJ, ruling on the lawfulness of national measures, provided that 'national measures liable to hinder or make less attractive the exercise of fundamental freedoms guaranteed by the Treaty must fulfil four conditions'. The Court then went on to list these conditions as follows:

- the rules must be applied in a non-discriminatory manner;
- they must be justified by imperative requirements in the general interest;
- they must be suitable for securing the attainment of the objective which they pursue;
- they must not go beyond what is necessary to attain it.

It can therefore be argued that a clear link has been established between the 'justification' of rules relating to free movement of goods, under *Cassis* and Art 30, and those relating to free movement of persons.

(3) THE FREEDOM TO PROVIDE SERVICES

Basic rights

While the right of establishment involves the setting up of a *permanent base* in a host State for an unspecified period, the right of free movement to provide services involves carrying out an economic activity, in a host State, for a *temporary period*, where the provider has no permanent base in that State.

The distinction is often difficult to draw, but this should not cause any concern as, as discussed above, the provisions can largely be read in parallel.

Article 49 of the EC Treaty prohibits measures which restrict the provision of services where the provider of the service is established in a *different Member State* to the recipient. Article 50 of the EC Treaty defines 'services' as those normally provided for remuneration, giving examples such as activities of an industrial or commercial character, activities of craftsmen and activities of the professions.

The ECJ has interpreted 'services' widely, including medical services, vocational training and tourism and it is likely to include any (lawful) temporary presence in another Member State, unless specifically covered by another area of the Treaty. Importantly, the Court has also held that the concept of services includes the right to *receive*, as well as provide, a service (Joined Cases 286/82 and 26/83, *Luisi* and *Carbone* and Case 186/87, *Cowan v Tresor Public*).

As those wishing to provide or receive a service do not wish to establish a permanent base in the host State, rights *do not include* residence rights for either the provider or receiver of a service or his/her family.

Protection from discrimination

Not surprisingly, Art 49 of the EC Treaty requires the elimination of all discrimination, based on nationality, against non-national providers of services. This article is supported by the more general Art 12 of the EC Treaty, which requires the elimination of discrimination based on nationality.

EXCEPTIONS TO THE RIGHT OF FREE MOVEMENT TO PROVIDE SERVICES

What does the Treaty say?

Article 55 of the EC Treaty specifically provides that the derogations found in Arts 45 and 46 of the EC Treaty, in relation to establishment, also apply to the freedom to move freely to provide (or receive) a service. Consequently, discussion provided above in relation to such derogations will be relevant.

Articles 39 (workers), 46 (establishment) and 55 (services) of the EC Treaty all contain derogation from the principle of free movement on grounds of public policy, public security and public health. Similarly, Arts 39, 45 and 55 of the EC Treaty also contain derogation on the basis of the exercise of official authority.

The attitude of the ECJ

Exceptions to the right of free movement have been interpreted restrictively by the Court. Exhaustive examination of the Court's approach is not possible or appropriate here. It is important, however, to extract recurrent themes which are to be found in the Court's judgments.

While legislation that affords rights to individuals has been widely interpreted, legislation that allows Member States to derogate has been narrowly interpreted, thus ensuring that restrictions on free movement are kept to a minimum. Unsurprisingly, this approach mirrors the Court's approach in relation to free movement of goods, discussed in Chapter 7.

ENFORCING RIGHTS IN RELATION TO FREE MOVEMENT OF PERSONS

In addition to understanding that Community law provides individuals with rights in relation to free movement throughout the Member States, it is also necessary to consider how such rights may be enforced.

If a Member State fails to comply with its obligations in relation to the free movement of persons within the EU, the Commission (or second Member State) may initiate enforcement proceedings against that State (Arts 226 and 227 of the EC Treaty).

In addition, the doctrine of direct effect allows individuals to enforce rights relating to free movement. The doctrine provides that Community law affords rights and obligations, not only to Member States but also to individuals and, importantly, that individuals may enforce their rights before national courts. Not all Community law has direct effect as certain conditions apply and it is therefore important to consider whether the above rules may be so enforced.

RIGHTS OF ESTABLISHMENT:

- Right exists in regard to natural and legal persons (Art 50) to set up under the same rules as for nationals (Art 43).
- National law must be followed UNLESS discriminatory (Arts 12 and 43)
- ECJ have interpreted 'discriminatory' very widely, includes direct and indirect discrimination (*Thieffry*) and even rules which although not discriminatory, place migrants at a disadvantage (*Stanton*)

Includes right to establish a business (Arts 43–48) or to provide a service (Arts 49–55) in a host State. ECJ has confirmed that there is much common ground between these rights and the rights of workers (*Royer*). Distinction between establishment and services is particularly indistinct

QUALIFICATIONS may be problematic. Consider Art 50:

- Harmonising legislation and mutual recognition
- Generally qualifications should be recognised (*Vlassopoulou*)

RIGHT TO PROVIDE A SERVICE IN A HOST STATE:

- Relates to temporary presence in host State
- 'Services' considered in Art 50, ECJ has interpreted rules widely to include those wishing *to receive* a service in a host State (*Cowan*)

Rights to free movement for the SELF EMPLOYED

FAMILIES wishing to accompany those establishing themselves in host state may do so under similar conditions to workers' families (Dir (73/148/EEC)). Rules may be applied by analogy to workers families

EXCEPTIONS: A similar thread exists with regard to the manner in which ECJ have interpreted and apply rules which limit free movement (*Walgrave v Koch*). Limits on freedom of establishment/provision of services (see Art 55 – services to be treated as establishment limitations):

- Exercise of official authority, consider as for 'public service' exception and workers (*Reyners*)
- Public policy, security, health as *per* Art 39(3) (*Walgrave v Koch*)

FREE MOVEMENT in Relation to ESTABLISHMENT and the PROVISION of SERVICES

Free movement of workers

The ECJ has been particularly concerned with emphasising that Art 39 of the EC Treaty provides rights to individuals. In Case 167/73, *Commission v France*, the *French Seamen* case, the Court held that Art 39 is *'directly applicable in the legal system of every Member State'*. In addition, it was provided that all conflicting national law should be rendered inapplicable. Furthermore, the Court has also made it clear that the Article places not only an obligation on the Member States to ensure the facilitation of free movement but also places a duty on individuals to do likewise (see, for example, Case C-415/93, *Bosman*).

Freedom of establishment

Case 2/74, *Reyners*, provides authority that Art 43 of the EC Treaty is directly effective.

Freedom to provide and receive services

Case 33/74, *Van Binsbergen*, provides authority the Art 49 of the EC Treaty has direct effect.

9 Competition Law

As we have already considered, the primary aim of the Community is the creation of a common market. This has meant that *all unnecessary barriers to trade must be removed*. The Community plays a part by, for example, ensuring the removal of all customs duties. In addition, Member States are obliged to ensure that national laws do not, amongst other things, create unnecessary pecuniary or quantitative restrictions to trade or hinder the free movement of persons within the Community.

While these activities contribute to the aim of integrating the economies of Member States they would not, alone, be sufficient to ensure the creation of a single market. The Treaty recognises that 'undertakings' (businesses of various types) also have their part to play in ensuring the creation of a common market.

Article 3(g) of the EC Treaty provides that one of the activities of the Community is to ensure that *'competition in the internal market is not distorted'*. The Community consequently provides undertakings with specific obligations relating to competition by virtue of Arts 81 and 82 of the EC Treaty. These Articles prohibit anti-competitive agreements and the abuse of a dominant market position respectively.

THE AIMS OF COMMUNITY COMPETITION LAW

The aims of EC Competition law are broad, complementing those of free movement of goods. While rules relating to free movement remove barriers to trade set up by Member States, EC competition law attempts to control the barriers to trade that may be set up by commercial undertakings. The primary aim of competition law can consequently be defined as aiding economic integration within the Community.

The rules relating to competition also fulfil other functions, including:

- consumer protection – rules on competition discourage price fixing, excessive charges, etc;
- efficiency – efficiency often suffers in a monopoly situation, but is normally encouraged by competition;
- fairness – the Preamble to the EC Treaty refers to *'fair competition'* and this can be seen to relate to areas such as the prohibition of government subsidies, etc, creating a healthy market/level playing field, where small as well as large firms may prosper.

The basis of EC competition rules

The rules contained in Arts 81 and 82 of the EC Treaty follow those established by the USA's Sherman Act 1890. This Act, which prohibits 'every contract, combination or conspiracy in restraint of trade' and 'the monopolisation of trade and commerce' and has been adopted in other countries, such as Canada, Ireland, Italy and Sweden. The Act, in effect, prohibits distortion of free competition resulting from collusion or other conduct between two or more undertakings and also from the predominant market power of one.

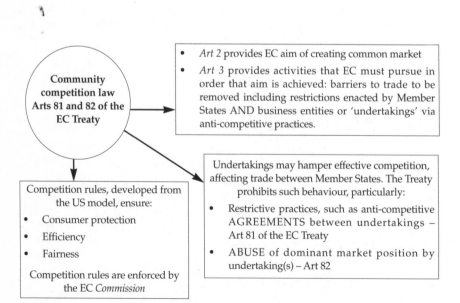

(1) THE PROHIBITION OF RESTRICTIVE PRACTICES (ART 81 OF THE EC TREATY)

Article 81 of the EC Treaty, in effect, prohibits undertakings from entering into anti-competitive agreements that may have a restrictive effect on inter-Community trade. The Article requires that such agreements be declared void, unless there is a sufficiently valid reason to allow them to be exempted by the Commission.

What does the Treaty say?

Article 81(1) of the EC Treaty prohibits 'All agreements between undertakings, decisions by associations of undertakings and concerted practices which may affect trade between Member States and which have as their object or effect the prevention, restriction or distortion of competition within the common market'. It then goes on to provide examples of the types of agreement that are prohibited.

In order to develop an understanding of the provisions contained within Art 81 of the EC Treaty, it is helpful to break the Article down into its constituent parts, namely:

- the types of agreement covered;
- the aims and/or effects of such agreements;
- the possible exemption of beneficial agreements.

As would be expected, Art 81 has been the subject of extensive interpretation by the European Court of Justice (ECJ):

'Agreements'

The term 'agreements' has been interpreted *widely and inclusively*. They have been held to include both formal and informal agreements, for example a gentleman's agreements (Cases 41, 44 and 45/69, *ACF Chemiefarma v Commission*, the *Quinine Cartel* case) and also unilateral contracts (Case 107/82R, *AEG-Telefunken v Commission*, where AEG refused to admit dealers to its dealership network). Agreements which are vertical (between producers and distributors) as well as horizontal (between, for example, producers) are caught by Art 81 of the EC Treaty (Case 56 and 58/64, *Consten and Grundig*).

To take any less broad a view of the type of agreements covered by Art 81 of the EC Treaty would leave a loophole through which less formal agreements could slip, leading to the distortion of competition within the Community.

In Case 193/83, *Windsurfing v Commission*, the Court explained that it is necessary to look at the *whole agreement* and it was held to be irrelevant that certain restrictions within the agreement do not affect trade.

'Undertakings'

The term 'undertaking' has also been interpreted widely to include every type of entity from a single individual to a multi-national corporation, provided they are capable of becoming engaged in economic activity (Case 41/90, *Hofner and Elsner v Macrotron*). The width of the term undertaking can be demonstrated by Commission Decision (78/516/EEC), *Re Unitel*, where it was provided that an opera singer was an undertaking for the purpose of competition rules.

The term has also been held to include *parent companies* established *outside the EC*. Such companies will be held responsible for acts of their subsidiaries within the EC (Case 48/69, *ICI v Commission*, the *Dyestuff* case and Cases C-89 etc/85, *Ahlstrom oy v Commission*, the *Woodpulp* case).

'Decisions by associations of undertakings'

This term has been held to incorporate trade associations and includes *non-binding recommendations* by such associations.

'Concerted practices'

Concerted practices were defined in the *Dyestuff* case as 'a form of co-ordination between undertakings which, without having reached the stage where an agreement properly so called has been concluded, knowingly substitutes practical co-operation between them for the risks of competition'.

No contract need exist, and the practice is more a type of behaviour than an agreement. In *Dyestuff*, it was accepted that what may appear to be price fixing at first sight can sometimes be 'oligopolistic interdependence' (that is, responding to movements in the market – such as oil companies responding to changes in competitors prices – with no actual collusion). The burden of proof is, however, on the defendant to demonstrate that there has been no collusion.

'Which may affect trade between Member States'

The need for 'inter-Community' effect

In situations where only trade *within* one Member State is affected, national law alone will apply as the Community will have no jurisdiction to act. (Case 61/80, *Co-operative Stremsel en Kleurselfabriek* and *Woodpulp*). Take care, however, that there is no *possibility* of affect, whether direct or indirect, on inter-Community trade

The nature of the effect on trade

The Court has held that there need be no actual effect on trade and that the *potential* for such an outcome is sufficient for an agreement to fall within Art 81 (Case 56/65, *Société Technique Miniere v Maschinenbau*, *STM*).

The Court has also held that it does not matter that the effect was not detrimental; indeed, in *Consten and Grundig*, the effect of the agreement was an increase in trade, but the agreement was still held to come within the scope of the competition rules.

The extent of the effect: the *de minimis* rule

Trade must be affected to an *appreciable extent* as Art 81(1) is subject to the *de minimis* rule. This can be explained by consideration of Case 5/69, *Volk v Vervaecke*. Volk had entered into an agreement which involved an exclusive distribution deal but as Volk produced less than 1% of washing machines within the relevant market, the agreement was considered to have no appreciable affect on trade.

The Commission issued guidance on what is appreciable, and what is not, in their *Notice on Minor Agreements 1986*. In the Commission's view (which is not binding on the ECJ), trade between Member States will not be affected to an appreciable extent if:

- the agreement concerns goods which do not represent more than 5% of the total market for such goods; *and*
- the total turnover of the undertakings involved is less that 2,000,000 Euros.

The 'object or effect' of the agreement

The Court has held that the 'object' of the agreement and the 'effect' of the agreement should be considered separately (*Consten and Grundig*).

Agreements whose *object* is anti-competitive

If the 'object' is found to be anti-competitive it will be *unnecessary* to consider the 'effect' as the agreement will automatically come within the scope of Art 81 of the EC Treaty.

Agreements whose object is *not* anti-competitive

The 'Rule of Reason'

The 'Rule of Reason' approach is commonly used in the USA, but it is questionable whether it is appropriate in the European context. Under this approach the reason for the agreement is considered and, if not anti-competitive, the agreement may be removed from the scope of Art 81 of the EC Treaty. There is, however, much academic debate as to how valuable the rule may be in deciding which agreements come within the scope of the Community's competition rules as, despite the best of motives, there may still be a restrictive affect on trade (see, for example, *Consten and Grundig* and Case 258/78, *Nungesser*).

The 'effect' of agreements

As considered above, where the object of an agreement is anti-competitive, that agreement will automatically be considered to be within the scope of Art 81. Where the object of the agreement is *not* anti-competitive unless the 'Rule of Reason' applies – which is unlikely bearing in mind the Court's jurisprudence – the '*effect*' of the agreement will have to be considered.

The 'prevention, restriction or distortion of competition within the common market'

The Treaty prohibits agreements which have as their effect the '*prevention, restriction or distortion of competition within the common market*' and then goes on to provide examples of such agreements.

A 'test' for behaviour amounting to market distortion was developed by the Court in *STM* where the Court explained that: '*It must be possible to foresee ... that the agreement in question may have an influence, direct or indirect, actual or potential, on the pattern of trade between Member States.*'

The Treaty provides that agreements which:

- involve price fixing or enforce other trading conditions;
- limit or control production, markets, technical development or investment;
- share markets or sources of supply;
- place parties at a disadvantage by applying dissimilar conditions to equivalent transactions; or
- require supplementary contracts to be concluded, as a term of the original agreement, where such a supplementary contract has no connection to the original agreement,

shall come within the scope of Art 81 of the EC Treaty.

The consequences of infringing Art 81(1) (Art 81(2) of the EC Treaty)

If an agreement is found to come within the scope of Art 81(1) of the EC Treaty, Art 81(2) of the EC Treaty provides that the agreement *'shall be automatically void'*. (It should be noted, however, that an exemption may be available under Art 81(3) of the EC Treaty, see below.)

Jurisdiction with regard to the *application* of Art 81(2) of the EC Treaty is shared between the Commission and the national courts (Case C-234/89, *Delimitis v Henninger Brau*), *although only the Commission may provide an exemption*.

In view of the Commission's monopoly with regard to the granting of exemptions, the national courts may only rule on whether an agreement is void where:

- the agreement *clearly* falls outside the scope of Art 81(1) of the EC Treaty; *or*
- the agreement *clearly* infringes Art 81(1) of the EC Treaty and there is no possibility of a an exemption being available.

It should be noted that where part of an agreement falls within the scope of Art 81(1) of the EC Treaty, it may be possible for the offending terms to be severed while leaving the rest of the agreement in tact. In the UK, this is known as the 'blue pencil' test.

The Commission has a major role in the policing and enforcement of the Community's competition rules, both under Art 81 and Art 82 of the EC Treaty. The Commission's powers are derived from the Council, under

Regulation (EEC) 17/62 and are discussed in further detail following consideration of Art 82 of the EC Treaty.

Exemptions to Art 81(2) (Art 81(3) of the EC Treaty)

Exemptions may only be granted by the Commission (*Delimitis*). The Commission may issue negative clearance, individual and block exemptions and comfort letters, all of which are considered, in turn, below.

(a)   Negative clearance

Undertakings may approach the Commission *before* entering into an agreement in order to ascertain whether or not such an agreement will breach Art 81(1). Agreements that are notified to the Commission can be provided with *negative clearance*, which is formal notification that the agreement does *not* fall within the scope of Art 81(1) of the EC Treaty as it is not anti-competitive.

Should an undertaking supply the Commission with false or misleading information, the undertaking may be fined and/or refused an exemption (Regulation (EEC) 17/62). Negative clearance is persuasive but not legally binding.

(b)   Individual and block exemptions

The Treaty, under Art 81(3) of the EC Treaty, provides that certain agreements although restrictive and within the scope of Art 81(1), may nevertheless gain an exemption which will result Art 81(2) being inapplicable.

The reason for such exemptions being available is that the Community recognises that certain agreements may have positive effects that outweigh any possible detrimental affect on trade. The Treaty lays down *four conditions* that must be satisfied before an exemption can be granted and the agreement must:

- improve the production or distribution of goods, or promote technical or economic progress; *and*

- allow consumers (that is members of the public and other undertakings) to enjoy a fair share of the resulting benefit; *while*

- not imposing restrictions on the undertakings which are unnecessary to the above objectives; *providing*

- it does not allow the undertaking the possibility of eliminating competition in respect of a substantial part of the products in question (usually agreements between undertakings with a large share of the market are considered as eliminating competition).

The Commission may provide one of *two types of exemption*, namely:

- individual; or
- group/block.

(i)   Individual exemptions

When undertakings notify the Commission of an agreement, the Commission may give the agreement an individual exemption under the above rules, in recognition of the agreements *positive* consequences. This will mean that the agreement falls within the scope of Art 81(1), *but* that it is being exempted.

(ii)   Block exemptions

Article 81(3) of the EC Treaty allows the Commission to declare categories of agreements to be exempt.

Acting under authority delegated by the Council, the Commission has issued a number of regulations in relation to agreements concerning, amongst other things, exclusive distribution (Regulation (EEC) 1983/83), exclusive purchasing (Regulation (EEC) 1984/83) and franchising (Regulation (EEC) 4087/88). These have had the effect of providing *certainty* for undertakings and *reducing the workload* of the Commission as agreements which come within the scope of a block exemption do not have to be notified to the Commission.

(c)   Comfort letters

While the use of block exemptions has gone some way to relieve the workload of the Commission in regard to the issue of exemptions the Commission does not, however, have sufficient resources to grant individual exemptions or negative clearance in any but the most pressing cases.

The Commission has therefore developed a system of what are known as *comfort letters* indicating that an exemption would be appropriate *if* an investigation had been continued. Comfort letters are not, however, legally binding on either national courts or the ECJ. It is also generally accepted that they are not susceptible to judicial review (see, for example, Case 99/79, *Lancôme v Etos*, which is one of the *Perfumes* cases).

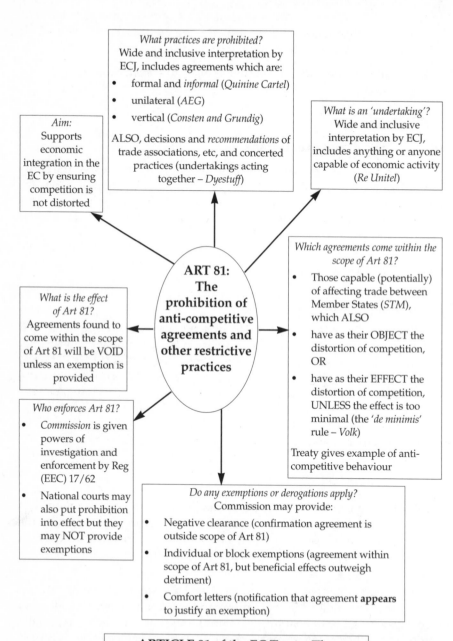

What practices are prohibited?
Wide and inclusive interpretation by ECJ, includes agreements which are:

- formal and *informal* (*Quinine Cartel*)
- unilateral (*AEG*)
- vertical (*Consten and Grundig*)

ALSO, decisions and *recommendations* of trade associations, etc, and concerted practices (undertakings acting together – *Dyestuff*)

What is an 'undertaking'?
Wide and inclusive interpretation by ECJ, includes anything or anyone capable of economic activity (*Re Unitel*)

Aim:
Supports economic integration in the EC by ensuring competition is not distorted

ART 81: The prohibition of anti-competitive agreements and other restrictive practices

Which agreements come within the scope of Art 81?

- Those capable (potentially) of affecting trade between Member States (*STM*), which ALSO
- have as their OBJECT the distortion of competition, OR
- have as their EFFECT the distortion of competition, UNLESS the effect is too minimal (the '*de minimis*' rule – *Volk*)

Treaty gives example of anti-competitive behaviour

What is the effect of Art 81?
Agreements found to come within the scope of Art 81 will be VOID unless an exemption is provided

Who enforces Art 81?

- *Commission* is given powers of investigation and enforcement by Reg (EEC) 17/62
- National courts may also put prohibition into effect but they may NOT provide exemptions

Do any exemptions or derogations apply?
Commission may provide:

- Negative clearance (confirmation agreement is outside scope of Art 81)
- Individual or block exemptions (agreement within scope of Art 81, but beneficial effects outweigh detriment)
- Comfort letters (notification that agreement **appears** to justify an exemption)

ARTICLE 81 of the EC Treaty: The Prohibition of Anti-Competitive Agreements

The Commission's discretion

It should be noted that Art 81(3) of the EC Treaty confers a great deal of discretion on the Commission. It has been argued that, of late, the Commission has used its position to encourage co-operation between larger firms in order to meet challenges from the American and Japanese markets. This may be compared to the Commission's earlier approach, which was to promote collaboration between smaller and medium sized undertakings, mitigate the effects of recession, etc.

(2)   ABUSE OF A DOMINANT MARKET POSITION (ART 82 OF THE EC TREATY)

Article 82 of the EC Treaty, like Art 81, seeks to prevent *undertakings* from becoming involved in anti-competitive behaviour. It does this by prohibiting *abuse*, by one or more undertakings, of a dominant market position within the Community. The Article goes on to provide examples of abusive behaviour. It should be understood at the outset that *the Article does not prohibit dominance*, merely the abuse of such a position within the European market place.

Art 82 of the EC Treaty provides that:

Any abuse by one or more undertakings of a dominant position within the common market or in a substantial part of it shall be prohibited as incompatible with the common market in so far as it may affect trade between Member States.

Once more consideration of decisions of the ECJ is very important to gaining an understanding of the extent and effect of the prohibition contained within the Treaty.

'One or more undertakings'

Article 82 of the EC Treaty refers to *'abuse by one or more undertakings'* of a dominant position. The term 'undertaking' has been interpreted in the same inclusive manner as for Art 81.

There has, however, been some disagreement as to whether collective or joint dominance should come within the scope of Art 81 or Art 82. While unilateral behaviour obviously comes within the scope of Art 82, the situation where two or more undertakings operate in a parallel manner is far less clear.

The ECJ appears to have rejected the possibility of oligopolies jointly enjoying a dominant position (Case 85/76, *Hoffman-La Roche v Commission*), suggesting that such agreements are more fittingly caught by Art 81.

The Commission's view apparently differs, as can be evidenced in Cases T-68 and 77–78/89, *Re Italian Flat Glass*, were the Commission concluded that three glass producers held a collective dominant position in the flat glass market. Academics have, however, argued that Art 82 will only apply where the behaviour of the undertakings is of the nature not to be caught by Art 81 of the EC Treaty.

'Dominant position'

While dominance itself is not prohibited, an undertaking must be shown to be dominant in a particular market before there can be any question of 'abuse'. It is therefore necessary to consider the following issues:

(1) the extent of the 'relevant market';

(2) the undertaking's 'dominance' of that market.

(1) The relevant market

Dominance can exist in both the supply and purchase of goods or services. The relevant market needs to be isolated before dominance can be assessed. This may be done by considering issues such as the availability of identical or interchangeable goods or services, the relevant territory or geographical influences and also temporal changes. Each needs to be considered in turn.

Isolating the relevant product or service

Consideration will need to be given to the product or service supplied or produced, including any products that are identical, equivalent, interchangeable or substitutable with those in question.

The leading case in this area is Case 27/76, *United Brands v Commission*. In *United Brands*, a major supplier of bananas in Europe, the Commission concluded that the relevant product market (RPM) was bananas.

The undertaking argued, however, that the RPM was fruit, as a rise in banana prices would result in a switch by consumers to other fruit (in economic jargon, the cross elasticity of *demand*). The ECJ concluded that the RPM was bananas, as a significant proportion of banana consumers where unable to switch to hard fruit (particularly the elderly, very young, infirm and, of course, the toothless!).

A further illustrative case on how the relevant market may be isolated is Case 6/72, *Europemballage and Continental Can v Commission* (*Continental Can*). Here it was argued that the undertaking held a dominant position with regard to the supply of metal containers for meat and fish products. While the Commission considered the extent to which consumers could switch to glass or plastic containers, the ECJ concluded that it was *also* necessary to consider how easily the manufacturers and suppliers of metal containers for vegetables could adapt their production processes to compete with Continental Can products (the cross-elasticity of *supply*).

It can therefore be concluded that when considering the extent of the RPM, 'interchangeability' is particularly important, both with regards to the *supply* of alternatives and consumer *demand* for such alternatives.

The relevant geographical market

Article 82 of the EC Treaty does not require that dominance be proven throughout the Community but it must be shown that it occurs in a '*substantial part of it*' for the Article to apply. The territories of individual Member States have been found to be a 'substantial part' of the EC, for example, Ireland in Cases C-241 and 242/91P, *RTE and ITP Commission*.

The relevant geographical market (RGM) of a product may be affected by such issues as the cost of transport and consumer taste and these issues should be taken into account when determining the RGM. Where goods are easily and relatively cheaply transportable, for example, the RGM may be considered to be the whole of the Community.

The relevant seasonal or temporal market

It should also be noted that it might, on occasion, also be necessary to consider the temporal market. In *United Brands*, for example, it was argued that the Commission should have considered that in summer bananas enjoy increased competition from 'summer' fruits.

Additional guidance on defining the relevant product market and geographic market can be found in the Commission Notice on the Defining of the Relevant Market for the Purposes of Community Competition Law (1997) OJ C372. While it is the Court who provides the definitive interpretation of such issues, the Commission's input is relevant as it is the Commission which enforces competition rules on behalf of the Community.

(ii) Dominance

Having ascertained the relevant market, it is then necessary to consider whether or not a particular undertaking is dominant in that market. It is consequently essential to consider what type of behaviour may indicate that an undertaking is dominant.

'Dominance' has been defined by the ECJ as 'a position of economic strength enjoyed by an undertaking which enables it to prevent competition being maintained on the relevant market by giving it the power to behave to an appreciable extent independently of its competitors, customers and ultimately of its consumers' (Case 27/76, *United Brands v Commission*).

This definition was extended in Case 5/85, *AKZO v Commission*, where the Court provided that dominance could also be evidenced by 'the power to exclude competition ... may also involve the ability to eliminate or seriously weaken existing competition or to prevent potential competitors from entering the market'.

Such decisions indicate that dominance involves an undertaking being sufficiently powerful so as to be able to act with little thought as to how its competitors, potential competitors or consumers, may react to its actions. A number of factors may bring about this situation, including the size of an undertaking's market share, the structure of the particular market and also obstacles to entering the market. Each will be considered in turn.

The relevance of market share in assessing dominance

The greater the size of an undertaking's market share, the greater the likelihood of dominance. While few undertakings will achieve 100% share of the market, an undertaking with a 70–80% share may be assumed sufficient to enjoy a dominant position (see, for example, *Continental Can*).

The relevance of market structure

Where market share is relatively low, it will be necessary to carry out a market analysis, involving consideration of the *market structure*. In *United Brands*, for example, market share was calculated to be between 40–45%. In addition to *United Brands'* market share, the market share of its nearest competitors was also considered. This was found to be 16% and, by comparison, *United Brands* was consequently considered to be dominant.

Obstacles to entering the market

Even if an undertaking enjoys a near monopoly situation, this need not always denote dominance. If it is relatively easy for competitors to enter the relevant market, the necessary autocracy is absent. The easier it is to enter the relevant market the more competitive the market will be seen to be.

Barriers to entry may include high investment costs, difficulty in obtaining raw materials or supplies, technical knowledge and distribution and where such problems are significant the market is likely to be dominated by existing participants.

'Abuse'

In order for Art 82 of the EC Treaty to apply, there must be 'abuse'. In Case 322/81, *Michelin v Commission*, the Court held that a firm in a dominant position has a 'special responsibility' not to allow its conduct to impair competition. 'Abuse' is an objective concept, and there is no need for the undertaking to have intended harm for particular behaviour to be considered abusive (*Hoffman-La Roche*).

The Treaty provides a non-inclusive list of abusive behaviour and, as the *United Brands* case provides an example of most of the abuses on the list, the case is essential reading! Other relevant cases include:

- imposing unfair prices – *Hoffman-La Roche* (granting of 'loyalty' discounts);
- predatory pricing – *AKZO* (part of a strategy to eliminate competition);
- Refusing to supply – Cases 6 and 7/73, *Commercial Solvents* (refusal to supply essential chemical to competitor);
- Supplying on discriminatory terms – *Michelin* (price discounts);
- Mergers/takeovers* – *Continental Can*.
- * Under Regulation (EEC) 4064/89, joint ventures such as mergers and takeovers must be notified to the Commission (subject to satisfaction of a turnover threshold of at least 2,500 m Euros). Under the Regulation, concentrations that are not cleared by the Commission will be considered to be illegal. Factors which will be taken into account by the Commission include the market share, market structure, obstacles to entry and also interests of the consumer (Commission Decision *Re Aerospatiale/Alexia/De Havilland* (Case IV/M/053) (1991)).

Exemption from Art 82 of the EC Treaty

There is *no exemption* available from the prohibition contained within Art 82 of the EC Treaty.

Undertakings may, however, obtain *negative clearance* (as already discussed in relation to Art 81 of the EC Treaty) if the Commission considers the undertaking's behaviour gives no grounds for action.

The Commission may also issue a *comfort letter* (also discussed above) if it considers Art 82 of the EC Treaty inapplicable with regard to the undertakings behaviour, thereby providing a degree of reassurance that their actions are acceptable to the Commission.

Enforcement of Arts 81 and 82 of the EC Treaty

(i)   By the Commission: Regulation (EEC) 17/62

Regulation (EEC) 17/62 gives the Commission its wide powers of investigation and enforcement with regard to Arts 81 and 82 of the EC Treaty.

The Commission, at its own instigation or following a complaint, may commence an investigation into a possible breach. The Commission has powers to enter the undertakings business premises, examine books and demand that any questions it asks be answered. Such investigations will normally take place with co-operation from appropriate national authorities.

The ECJ has held that where appropriate, an interim order may be available (Case 792/79R, *Camera Care Ltd v Commission*). Where a breach of competition rules is discovered, the Commission may make an order requiring that the breach be brought to an end.

In addition, where the breach is found to be either intentional or negligent, a fine may be imposed (up to one million Euros or 10% of the undertakings annual turnover, whichever is the greater).

It should be noted that a decision (other than the issue of a Comfort Letter) taken by the Commission with regard to the enforcement of EC competition law may be subject to judicial review (under Art 230 of the EC Treaty – see Chapter 6).

(ii)   By individuals: the direct effect of Arts 81 and 82 of the EC Treaty

Articles 81 and 82 of the EC Treaty have been held to be directly effective (Case 127/73, *BRT v SABAM*) although, as discussed above, national courts may not exempt agreements under Art 81(3) of the EC Treaty.

Abuse of a Dominant Market Position: Art 82 of the EC Treaty

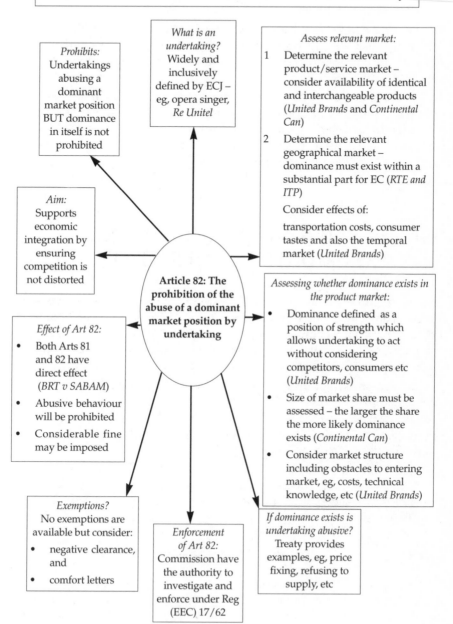

What is an undertaking? Widely and inclusively defined by ECJ – eg, opera singer, *Re Unitel*

Prohibits: Undertakings abusing a dominant market position BUT dominance in itself is not prohibited

Assess relevant market:

1 Determine the relevant product/service market – consider availability of identical and interchangeable products (*United Brands* and *Continental Can*)

2 Determine the relevant geographical market – dominance must exist within a substantial part for EC (*RTE and ITP*)

Consider effects of:

transportation costs, consumer tastes and also the temporal market (*United Brands*)

Aim: Supports economic integration by ensuring competition is not distorted

Article 82: The prohibition of the abuse of a dominant market position by undertaking

Assessing whether dominance exists in the product market:

• Dominance defined as a position of strength which allows undertaking to act without considering competitors, consumers etc (*United Brands*)

• Size of market share must be assessed – the larger the share the more likely dominance exists (*Continental Can*)

• Consider market structure including obstacles to entering market, eg, costs, technical knowledge, etc (*United Brands*)

Effect of Art 82:

• Both Arts 81 and 82 have direct effect (*BRT v SABAM*)

• Abusive behaviour will be prohibited

• Considerable fine may be imposed

Exemptions? No exemptions are available but consider:

• negative clearance, and

• comfort letters

Enforcement of Art 82: Commission have the authority to investigate and enforce under Reg (EEC) 17/62

If dominance exists is undertaking abusive? Treaty provides examples, eg, price fixing, refusing to supply, etc

This eases the Commission's already stretched resources but such means of enforcement is not problem free. In response, the Commission have issued guidance in its Notice on Co-operation between National Courts and the Commission (OJ 1993 C 39/6).

Where a competition case before a national court involves the question of the application of Community competition rules, the court may, of course, make use of the preliminary reference procedure under Art 234 of the EC Treaty (see Chapter 6).

National courts are free to apply an appropriate national remedy with respect to breaches of Community competition law (Case 45/76, *Comet v Produktschap*), providing that those remedies are effective (*Marshall No 2*), as discussed in Chapter 6. The ECJ has held that should a State authority breach competition rules, complainants may be able to gain damages under *Francovich* damages (Chapter 5).

(3) PUBLIC UNDERTAKINGS AND COMMUNITY COMPETITION RULES

It should be noted that both Arts 81 and 82 of the EC Treaty are addressed to undertakings as opposed to Member States. There is, however, nothing to prevent national authorities from becoming involved in commercial activity and, if competition rules are breached, the law will apply to the a authority in the same way as it does to other undertakings.

Government action may, in addition, reinforce anti-competitive behaviour in undertakings. Should this happen, the Community may make use of other Treaty articles such as Art 10 of the EC Treaty, which places an obligation on Member States to do nothing which may jeopardise the aims of the Treaty, to circumnavigate the problem.

The Treaty also provides Member States with certain obligations under Arts 86–89 of the EC Treaty. While outside the scope of this book, for the sake of completeness, it is necessary to be aware of the existence of these Treaty Articles.

Article 86 of the EC Treaty – State monopolies

Undertakings that enjoy 'special or exclusive rights' provided by the State would appear to be at odds with Community competition rules. Article 86 of the EC Treaty however, provides a balance between 'State monopolies' (such providers of water, gas electricity, railways, national lotteries, etc) and

Arts 81 and 82 of the EC Treaty by ensuring that the consequent restriction of competition is limited to that which is necessary and proportional to the aim being achieved (Case C-230/91, *Corbeau*).

Article 86(3) of the EC Treaty, provides the Commission with limited legislative powers in order to ensure the achievement of this aim.

Articles 87 to 89 of the EC Treaty – State aids

While the provision of State 'aid' (that is subsidies, loans on favourable terms, tax write-offs etc) to undertakings is not totally prohibited by the Treaty, aid which *'affects trade between Member States'* is *'incompatible with the common market'* (Art 87 of the EC Treaty).

The Treaty (Art 87(2) and (3) of the EC Treaty) goes on to provide a list of aid which is compatible with the common market and also provides the Commission with the obligation to keep any *existing* State aid under review (Art 88(1) of the EC Treaty). New aid must also be notified to the Commission under Art 88(3) of the EC Treaty.

While the latter provision is directly effective, other provisions relating to State aid are not and remain a matter for the Commission's discretion (Commission decisions are however subject to judicial review).

Any State aid that falls foul of the Treaty provisions may have to be repaid (Case 70/72, *Commission v Germany*).

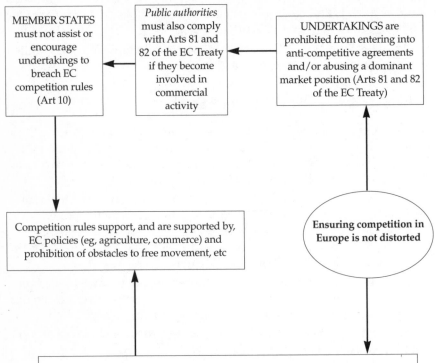

MEMBER STATES must not assist or encourage undertakings to breach EC competition rules (Art 10)

Public authorities must also comply with Arts 81 and 82 of the EC Treaty if they become involved in commercial activity

UNDERTAKINGS are prohibited from entering into anti-competitive agreements and/or abusing a dominant market position (Arts 81 and 82 of the EC Treaty)

Competition rules support, and are supported by, EC policies (eg, agriculture, commerce) and prohibition of obstacles to free movement, etc

Ensuring competition in Europe is not distorted

MEMBER STATES must also ensure healthy competition:

- Art 86 regulates State monopolies (such as public utilities). Restriction on competition is limited to what is necessary and proportionate (*Corbeau*)
- Arts 87–89 regulate State aid. State subsidies are generally prohibited as being incompatible with aims of the EC, although exceptions are available (Art 87 of the EC Treaty)

Rules Ensuring Competition in Europe is not Distorted

10 Revision and Examinations

This book is not intended to be a revision workbook or a guide on to how to pass exams but, very briefly, some hopefully helpful tips are provided below.

REVISION

Before you start, ensure that you are totally familiar with the syllabus of your course. Always plan your revision well in advance, ensuring that you start early enough to complete it *and* have time for relaxation. Trying to 'learn' European law by rote is boring, hard work and unlikely to produce good results. What you need to do is ensure you *understand* the law.

If you have worked consistently throughout your course you should have few worries. All you will need to do is ensure that what you have learned is at the forefront of your memory.

One of the most important things to do is discover what you do know and what areas need a little more work – there is little point in spending excessive time on areas that you are sufficiently familiar with! One of the best ways of testing your own knowledge is to get hold of past papers, old tutorial questions or even pick out appropriate questions from a revision workbook. Sit down and attempt to answer the questions – preferably in full and under similar constraints as will be imposed in the examination room. Check your answers and this should tell you which are your weak areas, allowing you the opportunity to concentrate your revision on these.

As touched upon above, there is little point in sitting down with your notes or textbook and trying to learn by rote. It is far more productive to read around the areas that you are having problems with, perhaps making you own notes, and then attempt to answer further questions, once more under examination conditions.

If you do make your own notes, which is always a good idea as it aids memory, make sure that they are not *too* detailed. If they are particularly detailed, you may find that there is little advantage in consulting them rather than a textbook, especially for last minute revision! You may also find it useful to use 'spider diagrams' or flow charts, which can also be useful when constructing answer plans.

EXAMINATION TECHNIQUE

Success (or failure) in examinations cannot be put down to good (or bad) examine technique. Without an appropriate level of knowledge and understanding, it is unlikely that exam success will be enjoyed. However, good exam technique can make the difference to achieving or just missing a grade.

Exam questions will either be 'essay type' or 'problem type'. While students often profess to only being able to cope with one type or the other, there is actually very little difference in what is required and both should be approached in the same way.

Always prepare an answer plan. You may feel that there is little time for such luxury in a time constrained assessment but in reality you will probably save time – unplanned answers often ramble and points may be repeated or irrelevant issues discussed. Your plan need not be long or complex; often a few key words, in an appropriate order, will be sufficient.

All answers should have an introduction, a 'main' part and a conclusion. An introduction can be seen as an opportunity to 'set the scene', provide relevant background information and/or demonstrate an understanding of how the subject matter of your answer relates to the wider view of Europe. Alternatively, if you find this difficult, the introduction can be used to explain to the reader what needs to be discussed, and why, in order to answer the question.

The 'main' part of your answer should contain the 'meat'. When planning your answer, you should not only decide what you need to say, but also the order in which it is most effectively said. This will ensure that your answer flows.

The exam question will require that you reach a conclusion. Never forget to do this. You may have been asked to advise someone, consider a proposition or comment on the development of law, for example. To ensure that you have actually answered the question asked (not the one you would like to have been asked), *always* re-read the question before embarking on your conclusion. If you discover that you have wandered from the point or missed something important, you will then still have the opportunity to put matters right.

Don't make any new points in your conclusion and don't be tempted to repeat arguments. It is often sufficient to say: 'In conclusion, based on the arguments (or discussion or facts) provided above, I would advise Joe that ...'

As well as planning your answers, don't forget to plan your time. Most undergraduate examinations are three hours in length; some have additional 'reading time'. Divide this time carefully between the number of questions that have to be answered and ensure that you don't spend too long on one answer to the detriment of the others.

It is *very* important to ensure that you answer the requisite number of questions. If you are required, for example, to answer four questions, you will not attain as many marks by answering three questions particularly well as you could by answering the required four reasonably well.

I hope that it is unnecessary to remind you to check the date, time and place of the examination! Do, however, ensure that you are aware of what you may take into the examination room with you. For example, it is often possible to take in a clean copy of EC legislation – which you should find invaluable if you have referred to it diligently throughout your course.

All that remains now is to wish you every success!

Index